Inflation

Other Books of Related Interest

Opposing Viewpoints Series

Reforming Wall Street

At Issue Series

What Is the Future of the US Economy?

Current Controversies Series

The World Economy

> "Congress shall make no law ... abridging the freedom of speech, or of the press."

First Amendment to the US Constitution

The basic foundation of our democracy is the First Amendment guarantee of freedom of expression. The Opposing Viewpoints Series is dedicated to the concept of this basic freedom and the idea that it is more important to practice it than to enshrine it.

Inflation

Noah Berlatsky, Book Editor

GREENHAVEN PRESS
A part of Gale, Cengage Learning

Detroit • New York • San Francisco • New Haven, Conn • Waterville, Maine • London

Elizabeth Des Chenes, *Director, Publishing Solutions*

© 2013 Greenhaven Press, a part of Gale, Cengage Learning

Gale and Greenhaven Press are registered trademarks used herein under license.

For more information, contact:
Greenhaven Press
27500 Drake Rd.
Farmington Hills, MI 48331-3535
Or you can visit our Internet site at gale.cengage.com.

For product information and technology assistance, contact us at:

Gale Customer Support, 1-800-877-4253.
For permission to use material from this text or product, submit all requests online at www.cengage.com/permissions.

Further permissions questions can be emailed to permissionrequest@cengage.com.

Articles in Greenhaven Press anthologies are often edited for length to meet page requirements. In addition, original titles of these works are changed to clearly present the main thesis and to explicitly indicate the author's opinion. Every effort is made to ensure that Greenhaven Press accurately reflects the original intent of the authors. Every effort has been made to trace the owners of copyrighted material.

Cover Image © Hemera/Thinkstock/Getty Images.

LIBRARY OF CONGRESS CATALOGING-IN-PUBLICATION DATA

Inflation / Noah Berlatsky, book editor.
  p. cm. -- (Opposing viewpoints)
  Includes bibliographical references and index.
  ISBN 978-0-7377-6426-0 (hardcover) -- ISBN 978-0-7377-6427-7 (pbk.)
  1. Inflation (Finance) I. Berlatsky, Noah.
  HG229.I444894 2012
  332.4'1--dc23
                                                        2012016627

Printed in the United States of America
1 2 3 4 5 6 7 16 15 14 13 12

Contents

Chapter 1: What Causes Inflation?

Chapter 2: Is Inflation Dangerous?

Chapter 3: What Inflationary Conditions Pose the Greatest Threat to the US Economy?

Why Consider Opposing Viewpoints?

> *"The only way in which a human being can make some approach to knowing the whole of a subject is by hearing what can be said about it by persons of every variety of opinion and studying all modes in which it can be looked at by every character of mind. No wise man ever acquired his wisdom in any mode but this."*
>
> *John Stuart Mill*

In our media-intensive culture it is not difficult to find differing opinions. Thousands of newspapers and magazines and dozens of radio and television talk shows resound with differing points of view. The difficulty lies in deciding which opinion to agree with and which "experts" seem the most credible. The more inundated we become with differing opinions and claims, the more essential it is to hone critical reading and thinking skills to evaluate these ideas. Opposing Viewpoints books address this problem directly by presenting stimulating debates that can be used to enhance and teach these skills. The varied opinions contained in each book examine many different aspects of a single issue. While examining these conveniently edited opposing views, readers can develop critical thinking skills such as the ability to compare and contrast authors' credibility, facts, argumentation styles, use of persuasive techniques, and other stylistic tools. In short, the Opposing Viewpoints Series is an ideal way to attain the higher-level thinking and reading skills so essential in a culture of diverse and contradictory opinions.

In addition to providing a tool for critical thinking, Opposing Viewpoints books challenge readers to question their own strongly held opinions and assumptions. Most people form their opinions on the basis of upbringing, peer pressure, and personal, cultural, or professional bias. By reading carefully balanced opposing views, readers must directly confront new ideas as well as the opinions of those with whom they disagree. This is not to argue simplistically that everyone who reads opposing views will—or should—change his or her opinion. Instead, the series enhances readers' understanding of their own views by encouraging confrontation with opposing ideas. Careful examination of others' views can lead to the readers' understanding of the logical inconsistencies in their own opinions, perspective on why they hold an opinion, and the consideration of the possibility that their opinion requires further evaluation.

Evaluating Other Opinions

To ensure that this type of examination occurs, Opposing Viewpoints books present all types of opinions. Prominent spokespeople on different sides of each issue as well as well-known professionals from many disciplines challenge the reader. An additional goal of the series is to provide a forum for other, less known, or even unpopular viewpoints. The opinion of an ordinary person who has had to make the decision to cut off life support from a terminally ill relative, for example, may be just as valuable and provide just as much insight as a medical ethicist's professional opinion. The editors have two additional purposes in including these less known views. One, the editors encourage readers to respect others' opinions—even when not enhanced by professional credibility. It is only by reading or listening to and objectively evaluating others' ideas that one can determine whether they are worthy of consideration. Two, the inclusion of such viewpoints encourages the important critical thinking skill of objectively evaluating an author's credentials and bias. This evaluation will illuminate an author's reasons for taking a particular stance on an issue and will aid in readers' evaluation of the author's ideas.

It is our hope that these books will give readers a deeper understanding of the issues debated and an appreciation of the complexity of even seemingly simple issues when good and honest people disagree. This awareness is particularly important in a democratic society such as ours in which people enter into public debate to determine the common good. Those with whom one disagrees should not be regarded as enemies but rather as people whose views deserve careful examination and may shed light on one's own.

Thomas Jefferson once said that "difference of opinion leads to inquiry, and inquiry to truth." Jefferson, a broadly educated man, argued that "if a nation expects to be ignorant and free . . . it expects what never was and never will be." As individuals and as a nation, it is imperative that we consider the opinions of others and examine them with skill and discernment. The Opposing Viewpoints Series is intended to help readers achieve this goal.

David L. Bender and Bruno Leone,
Founders

Introduction

> "When I arrived in Rio de Janeiro
> on October 14 [1989], the official
> government rate of exchange was
> five Brazilian cruzados to one United
> States dollar. But on the black market
> [which means everywhere except at
> the Brazilian Central Bank], the rate
> was 9.5 cruzados to the dollar. By
> the time I left Brazil at the end of the
> month, the black market rate had gone
> down to 12.7 cruzados to the dollar, a
> 33 percent depreciation of the currency
> in just over two weeks!"
>
> Richard M. Ebeling, "On the
> Edge of Hyperinflation in Brazil,"
> Freedom Daily, March 1990.

Brazil has a long, mixed relationship with high inflation. During the 1960s and 1970s, Brazil had a very high average inflation rate. From 1960 to 1969 its rate was 45.8 percent. From 1970 to 1979 it was 30.5 percent. According to Ha-Joon Chang in his 2011 book *23 Things They Don't Tell You About Capitalism*, this high inflation rate did not damage Brazil's growth. On the contrary, he says, Brazil's per capita income increased at 4.5 percent during this period, making it "one of the fastest-growing economies in the world" at that time.

Chang concludes that Brazil's experience shows that "fairly high inflation is compatible with rapid economic growth." Economist Caio Megale, in a May 18, 2007, article in the *Zimbabwe Independent* added that inflation was seen as directly linked to growth—or, in Megale's words, as "the undesired consequence of economic development." Brazilians did not want such high inflation, but they were willing to tolerate it because it seemed to be, in part, a cost of their economic boom. In fact, the Brazilian government was financing growth in large part by printing money, which increased the money supply and contributed to inflation. In order to help people cope with this inflation, the government made adjustments like indexing salaries to inflation. Thus, as prices rose, wages automatically went up as well—which helped contribute to further inflation.

The policy of growth and inflation worked well for Brazil until the 1980s. At that time, world oil prices spiked, and droughts and floods increased food prices. As a result, inflation began to accelerate. Between 1980 and 1985, inflation averaged around 142 percent. From 1986 to 1989, it averaged a whopping 795.6 percent. In a February 22, 2002 article on the website of Pontificia Universidade Católica do Rio de Janeiro Leslie Evans describes the impact of this high inflation rate on Brazilians:

> Imagine that your rent doubled every 10 weeks. That your credit card charged 25% a month interest. That food and clothes went up 40% a month. That the value of your savings declined 2000% in a year! This was Brazil for ten years, from 1987 to 1997.

Brazil's inflation is an example of hyperinflation, or runaway inflation, and it had a devastating effect on the country's economy. Because the value of money dropped so rapidly, no one saved; everyone tried to spend as quickly as possible. Moreover, as prices skyrocketed, people only had money to spend on essentials, which badly hurt the economy.

The Brazilian government tried numerous plans to reduce inflation such as putting a ceiling on the money supply, so the government could not print too many bills. However, with the economy so damaged, people were buying less and less. Demand contracted faster than the money supply. Thus, inflation kept going up.

In 1993, Fernando Henrique Cardoso became Brazil's finance minister and oversaw the creation of a plan that gave the Brazilian central bank independence from political influence. The central bank instituted numerous bank reforms and froze wages so that they were no longer indexed to the spiraling inflation. The central bank also raised the cost of money by bumping up interest rates. Eventually interest rates reached 10–12 percent a year, which were among the highest in the world. Because of these changes, price levels dropped dramatically, and by 1997 Brazil's inflation was down to 7.1 percent, marking the end of hyperinflation.

Though Brazil overcame its lengthy battle with high inflation, experts disagree about the meaning of the country's accomplishment. Gustavo Franco, former president of Brazil's central bank, argues that the steps taken were necessary and justified going around the democratic process. Chang, on the other hand, points out that Brazil's growth rate has fallen substantially since it conquered inflation. Since 1997, Brazil has grown at a per capita rate of 1.3 per cent, far below the level it sustained in the 1960s and '70s.

Brazil is not alone in its struggle with inflation; inflation is an issue that impacts countries around the globe. *Opposing Viewpoints: Inflation* explores inflation further in the following chapters: What Causes Inflation?, Is Inflation Dangerous?, and What Inflationary Conditions Pose the Greatest Threat to the US Economy? Authors present varying perspectives on the benefits and dangers of inflation as well as its role in the global economy.

OPPOSING
VIEWPOINTS®
SERIES

| What Causes Inflation?

Chapter Preface

War is often cited as a cause of inflation. Economist James K. Galbraith argues in an April 20, 2004 article on *Salon*, that wars are usually financed by inflation:

"The big reason is that wars must be paid for, somehow. They require resources that civilians would otherwise use. Those resources must be diverted to the war effort. Usually, inflation is the easiest way."

Galbraith says the US government borrows to finance wars. Then the central bank increases the money supply, driving inflation up so that the value of the debt decreases (inflation means that money, including debt, is worth less). US Representative Ron Paul argues in a January 30, 2007, article on Antiwar.com:

> Congress and the Federal Reserve Bank have a cozy, unspoken arrangement that makes war easier to finance. Congress has an insatiable appetite for new spending, but raising taxes is politically unpopular. The Federal Reserve, however, is happy to accommodate deficit spending by creating new money through the Treasury Department. . . . The result of this arrangement is inflation. And inflation finances war.

In *The American Economy: A Historical Encyclopedia*, Cynthia L. Clark notes that the US Civil War, World Wars I and II, and Vietnam all saw "significant inflation." Clark says that in the era of metal coins, governments would lower the amount of precious metal in each coin, reducing the "purity" of the coins and essentially making money cheaper. In the era of paper money, the government could simply print more bills so that, again, money became worth less. This practice allowed governments to spend the huge amounts of money needed in wartime without directly taxing the populace. Instead inflation served as an indirect tax and people's wages fell in real terms.

This kind of war financing was less obvious and more politically acceptable.

War financing is not the only cause of inflation. The viewpoints in the following chapter offer varying opinions on the factors that cause inflation.

"Markets are people, and the
preferences of those people, for good or
bad, end up in the prices we see."

What Are the Causes
of Inflation?

John T. Harvey

John T. Harvey is a professor of economics at Texas Christian University. In the following viewpoint he argues that inflation is not caused by an increase in the money supply. Rather, he says, inflation occurs when a producer controls a significant amount of a good and deliberately raises the price. The price of a good may also go up, Harvey says, if there is an increase in demand for a good or a sudden decrease in supply. In cases like these, Harvey concludes, the Federal Reserve increases the money supply to accommodate the demand for more money caused by inflation.

As you read, consider the following questions:

1. Why does Harvey say that the money supply rose during the inflation of the 1970s and 1980s?
2. According to Harvey, who benefits when a financial asset drives up the price of a good?
3. What example does Harvey give of a supply shock?

Inflation is simply a rise in the average price of goods and services in the macroeconomy. Which particular goods and services depends on the measure we are examining. Consumer price inflation is the one usually in the news, and it takes a weighted average of various items purchased by the typical household (the list being determined by survey and then updated periodically). The average can rise while some prices have actually fallen, and how much it reflects your personal situation is a function of how closely the basket of goods and services in the index matches your buying patterns. But, the bottom line is that we say that inflation has occurred when the average price of those goods and services has increased.

Inflation Defined

This does not happen by magic. It takes someone, somewhere making a conscious choice to charge more for the good or service they sell. The initial increase does not have to be in something that is being directly measured by the consumer price index. No household in my neighborhood, for example, buys barrels of oil; and yet when they become more expensive that sends a ripple throughout all related products. In the end, consumer prices jump as well.

Of course, that someone, somewhere who raises their price must also be in a position to make it stick. I could march into the Chancellor's office here at TCU [Texas Christian University] and demand that my salary be doubled, but that probably won't accomplish a whole lot (other than to give me a chance to update my vita [an academic resume] while I am cleaning out my office). Other factors must come into play. Many circumstances can cause inflation. I will focus on four.

Causes of Inflation: Market Power

First, the economic agent could have *market power*. This means they have the ability to avoid (at least to some extent) competitive pressures. It is the latter that forces firms to please consumers.

Adam Smith [economist] wrote in 1776 that we cannot trust the undertakers of business to look out for anyone but themselves, and so we must handcuff them. But not with markets, per se, with competition, and the two do not always go hand in hand. The OPEC [Organization of the Petroleum Exporting Countries] oil cartel in the 1970s and 1980s is a classic example of market power. Had there been other viable sources of what they sold, they could not have restricted supply and driven up prices as they did because the competition would not have allowed them to do so. We would have just bought oil (or a close substitute) from someone else. Up to late 1973, they lacked the political will to set strict quotas among the various exporters. But, once the motivation was provided by US involvement in the Yom Kippur War [the United States sided with Israel against Arab nations, including many members of OPEC], they made a conscious decision to raise prices by cutting supply. And because they were able to avoid competition, it worked! Even though households do not buy barrels of oil, it caused terrible inflation. It drove up the prices of anything that used petroleum or petroleum-based products, it raised the price of gas and, therefore, anything that needed to be transported, and it caused inflation in other energy sources as users shifted to those products. Market power—not money growth—caused this inflation. The money supply only rose as a result of the fact that firms and consumers took out larger loans and sold assets for cash. The Federal Reserve [the US central bank] acted as it should have done in these circumstances, accommodating this increased demand.

(Note that having market power does not give carte blanche to raising prices. Even monopolists can only charge so much before consumers stop buying their products. However, they have the incentive and ability to engage in periodic attempts to capture more income for themselves. I won't go into the specifics of when and how they do so here, but this phenomenon is discussed in detail in Alfred Eichner's classic study of the microeconomy, *Megacorp and Oligopoly: Micro Foundations of Macro Dynamics*,

Cambridge U Press, 1976. Though it's a little dated, the basic lessons still apply.)

The impact of the inflation of the 1970s and 1980s was hardly even, and this is always the case. Remember that when you pay more for something, the person on the other side of the register is also getting more. It depends on individual buying patterns and particularly where you earn your salary. With the OPEC inflation, those in the oil industry, while facing the same rising prices at the gas pump, grocery store, etc., as everyone else, were actually better off than they had been before because their salaries and profits rose at a higher rate. This was especially true of those in the OPEC countries who controlled the oil supplies. The inflation process redistributed income towards them—that was the whole point, wasn't it? This fact is exceedingly important to understand. Inflation never affects everyone equally. It shifts buying power from one group to another (even though the winners may still complain because they see themselves as hurt by the overall price increases—what they don't understand is their role in causing the latter!). In fact, it is the very attempt to capture more income that is at the heart of the inflationary process under these circumstances. Money supply growth did not cause prices to rise, OPEC's attempt to grab a larger income share did. No amount of controlling the money supply was going to eliminate the ultimate impact of rising oil prices: the redistribution of income towards those countries and the oil industry.

As a very quick aside, it's worth pointing out that just because the market created a particular price, wage, profit rate, or income does not mean that it is somehow objectively "fair." These numbers only quantify our existing social values. There are, of course, more purely economic forces at work, too. Gold is more valuable than silver because there is less of it. But can we truly justify the wages and incomes earned by African Americans in the 1950s as economically reasonable, simply a function of their productivity? The fact of the matter is that a free-market system in a racist

Inflation Rates, 1970s vs. 2000s

Inflation rates in the 1970s were much higher than in the 2000s, in part because oil suppliers in the 1970s deliberately restricted supply, forcing prices up.

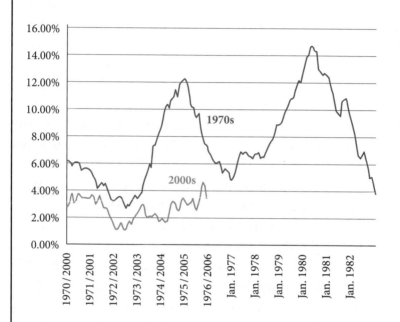

TAKEN FROM: Timothy McMahon, "Inflation Similarities Between the 2000s and the 1970s," InflationData.com, April 21, 2006.

society reflects and reinforces racist values. Markets are people, and the preferences of those people, for good or bad, end up in the prices we see. My point here is that there may be times when we would, as a nation, actually prefer to alter the outcomes created by competitive pressures. Desegregation interfered with the market mechanism and the forces of competition, as did movements aimed at creating safer workplaces. Furthermore, paying African Americans more and reducing the chances of on-the-job injuries caused inflation (because they raised costs) and redistributed income. Was this justifiable or not? Unfortunately, these are not simple questions.

Causes of Inflation: Demand Pull

Another means by which inflation can take place is a *rise in demand relative to supply*. Say there is an increase in the demand for housing during an economic expansion. Bottlenecks may arise in certain building supplies like lumber. Contractors bid up these prices in an attempt to secure the materials they need; these price increases then ripple through the economy. Firms and consumers again desire a larger money supply to be able to operate, which the Fed presumably accommodates. The producers of lumber and bricks may also experience a rise in their incomes as part of this process—and why shouldn't they? This is how a market system is supposed to work. Those selling goods and services in highest demand should see their profits and wages rise, even though by definition this will almost certainly cause inflation. This attracts others to sell these same goods and services, while some consumers go in search of substitutes. This is the greatest strength of a market system, its flexibility in the face of unanticipated changes.

Causes of Inflation: Asset Market Boom

Third and very relevant today [2011], *inflation can be injected from the asset market*.[1] The connection between the prices of goods and services and those of financial assets is tenuous. Sometimes there is practically none at all. Witness the 1990s, with a massive increase in stock prices but very little movement in the consumer price index. However, lines of causation can exist, particularly through commodities futures. I have already written about this at length in the context of gas prices:

Why You Are Paying So Much For Gas. The gist of the above is this. When speculative money[2] bids up the price of a commodity future, this creates an incentive for those actually selling the commodity to withhold supply today in favor of the future (when prices will presumably be higher). The rising spot price then convinces the speculator that her bet had been correct, and she increases her position. This may drive futures prices even higher, and so on. Thus, a goods price is driven up by the price of a financial asset. The winners here are 1) those whose portfolios include those assets (of course, they can only realize their gain by selling) and 2) the producers of the commodities in question. Those producers often bear the brunt of the blame for these inflations, but they are not actually the source. As usual with inflation, it leads to a rise in the money supply as agents take out loans and sell government securities. The way to stop this inflation is not via blocking monetary growth, however, but to control the link between the asset market and the commodity price.

Causes of Inflation: Supply Shock

Last is a *supply shock*. If a storm rages through the Gulf of Mexico, taking out oil derricks and refineries along the way, this may well raise the price of oil and gas. As it should, for this creates incentives to build more derricks and refineries and for consumers to find alternate energy sources. Again, this is what capitalism is supposed to do. In terms of who wins with this sort of inflation, it's obviously more complex since it depends on whose derricks were destroyed and who gets to build new ones. In any event, this, too, can lead to a rise in the money supply and there is no logical reason for the Fed to block this.

No Simple Equation Exists for the Cause of Inflation

This is not an all inclusive list, but I would think that it covers the vast majority of what we have experienced since the end of WWII (today, we are most threatened by the link between financial markets and commodities). The bottom line is that there are a number of processes that can create inflation, none of which starts with, "the money supply increases." Someone makes a conscious decision to raise a price or wage, and they must be able to make this stick. Because every higher price you pay means someone is getting more income, inflation causes a redistribution of income. Sometimes it does so in a manner that we would endorse and sometimes not. But in any event, it causes a rise in the demand for money that the Fed will almost certainly accommodate—and rightfully so, for refusing to do so almost always serves to punish those already in the weakest position.

I'm afraid this more realistic perspective does not offer a nice, simple rule as in the money growth ==> inflation camp. That said, neither do [other perspectives] since that's not how the world really works! In reality, monetary policy does not cause inflation, and it is not well placed to stop it. What it does do is very strongly and directly affect interest rates. But prices are determined elsewhere in the system.

Notes

1. That is, when stock prices increase, inflation can also increase.
2. Speculative money is money such as that placed in the stock market as a bet on the rise or fall of the price of goods.

*"Without a continuing increase in
the quantity of money, there can be
no inflation."*

Inflation Is Caused by an
Increase in the Money Supply

Howard Baetjer Jr.

*Howard Baetjer Jr. is a lecturer in economics at Towson University.
In the following viewpoint, he argues that the only cause of inflation is an increase in the money supply. In some cases, he says,
factors such as a decrease in supply may bid up a particular good
(like oil). However, he argues, if the money supply stays the same,
the increase in price of one good will be matched by a decrease in
prices of other goods. The only way that inflation can occur across
an entire economy, he concludes, is if the Federal Reserve decides to
increase the money supply.*

As you read, consider the following questions:

1. What does Baetjer say would happen to prices if you were
to cast a money-doubling spell?

Howard Baetjer Jr., "Something Besides Money Growth Causes Inflation?: The Root Cause
of Inflation Is a Settled Matter for Most Economists," *Freeman*, Foundation for Economic
Education, Inc., vol. 57, no. 6, July 2007. www.fee.org; www.thefreemanonline.org. All
rights reserved. Reproduced by permission.

2. If the supply of money does not increase and oil prices go up, what does Baetjer say should happen to the price of clothing?
3. According to Baetjer, what is the relationship between economic downturns and inflation?

Some economic phenomena can result from a variety of causes. A temporary increase in unemployment, for example, might be caused by a sudden, disruptive change in production technology, or in trade patterns, or in labor or tax laws; or it could be caused by natural disasters or wars, or by recessions due to monetary or fiscal policy. In such cases the exact cause is unclear.

Inflation Has One Cause

By contrast, a few economic phenomena have one and only one root origin; when we see the effect, we can be sure of the cause. One of these is inflation. Its root cause is a settled matter for most economists. In the words of the great Milton Friedman, whose masterwork with Anna Schwartz, *A Monetary History of the United States*, [1963] did a lot to settle the matter, "Inflation is always and everywhere a monetary phenomenon."

Unfortunately, many educated commentators have not learned this important truth. One of these is Robert Samuelson, who wrote in the *Washington Post* ("The Upside of Recession?" April 25 [2007]) that government subsidies can increase inflation and that recessions can reduce it. But that ain't so.

To understand Friedman's aphorism, let us consider this thought experiment: Suppose tonight, as we sleep, Harry Potter flies across the country and waves his magic wand to cast a money-doubling spell. The spell has no effect on the amount of goods and services; it affects only money. Every nickel becomes a dime, every quarter becomes a 50-cent piece, every dollar becomes two, every ten-dollar bill becomes a twenty, every checking account doubles its balance—in short, the money supply doubles overnight. What would we expect to happen to prices over the next day or two?

Even if no one knew that everybody else's money holdings had also increased, we would expect to see prices rise very fast as sellers discover that they can charge more for their goods than they could yesterday. Picture automobile dealerships. As people perceived an apparent sudden increase in their "wealth"—it's not wealth, it's just money, but they don't know that yet—many of them would head out excitedly to buy a new car. The dealerships would see many more customers than yesterday, all willing to pay much more than yesterday. The dealers would quickly raise their prices, realizing that they can charge more for their cars (which are no more numerous than yesterday). A similar process would occur at every store, market, online retailer, and real-estate agency in the land, and soon the price of just about everything would (to oversimplify a bit) approximately double.

The experiment illustrates the core of Friedman's insight—the general level of prices is a consequence of the money supply.

Now, would we say that Harry Potter had caused inflation? No, not if we use the term precisely. Inflation is a continuing increase in the level of prices, whereas the money-doubling spell would cause only a one-time doubling of prices. If Harry uses the spell only once, and nothing else increases the money supply, then we should expect prices to stabilize after their one-time jump. (Or, rather, in a healthy and innovative economy in which entrepreneurs continually figure out ways to cut costs and produce ever-greater abundance of goods and services, we should expect prices overall to decrease gradually. After all, with ever-increasing amounts of stuff to buy, and a fixed quantity of money to buy it with, everything should sell for less and less as time passes.)

If Harry Potter wanted to cause inflation—a continuing increase in the level of prices—he would have to cast a money-increase spell and leave it on so that more money would be created every night. Without a continuing increase in the quantity of

Milton Friedman

One of the premiere economists in the late 20th century, Milton Friedman's economic policies were favored by many country leaders, including President Ronald Reagan of the United States, Prime Minister Margaret Thatcher of the United Kingdom, and military dictator Augusto Pinochet of Chile. His 30-year tenure at the University of Chicago ushered in a new school of economic thought that produced several scholars and economic leaders who went on to win Nobel prizes. Friedman himself would win the Nobel Prize in 1976. Allan H. Meltzer, an economic scholar at Carnegie Mellon University, told the *Los Angeles Times*, "He was a great man. It's hard to think of anybody who never held a government position of any importance who influenced our country— and the whole world—as much as he did."

Before Friedman, many governments subscribed to the policies of British economist John Maynard Keynes, who believed that government should be involved in the ebb and flow of its economy. Friedman, however, wanted less government involvement. His free-market or laissez-faire policies were put into practice by both the U.K. and U.S. governments, though Keynes also continued to be an important influence on policy.

Friedman's commitment to limited government reached beyond the economy. He was on the board that recommended the end of using a draft in times of war. Friedman wanted to legalize drugs and prostitution. He also spoke against licensing boards, including the issuance of driver's licenses.

"Milton Friedman, American Economist
(1912–2006)," Newsmakers.
Detroit: Gale, 2008.

money, there can be no inflation. This is what Milton Friedman meant by his memorable aphorism.

Central Banks Cause Inflation

A consequence of this insight exposes the mistake made by Robert Samuelson and many others. Anything that does not continually increase the money supply can not cause inflation.

So what does cause inflation? Well, what or who increases the money supply? Central banks do. In the United States, the Federal Reserve System (the Fed) controls the money supply and thereby causes any inflation that occurs.

Let us look at some of Samuelson's specific points. He implies that high oil prices are driving inflation when he writes, "We all know about oil. Prices are about $60 a barrel," and he asserts that government spending drives inflation when he writes, "[T]he government's subsidies for corn-based ethanol are worsening inflation." Samuelson is surely correct that government should not subsidize ethanol and thereby push up the prices of corn and all things made with corn. But high oil prices and government spending on ethanol do not change the money supply, so they cannot change the level of prices.

Surely higher prices for oil and corn drive up the prices of goods and services produced using oil and corn, such as transportation and many foods, so we should expect to see higher price levels in those sectors of the economy. But inflation is an increase in the prices overall, not in just some sectors. If the prices of transportation and food rise, then the prices of other goods and services must fall unless more money flows into the system. If we have no more to spend in toto, then when we must spend more money on gasoline, we have less money to spend on, say, clothing. This means that clothing makers would have to lower their prices in order to sell their wares; they in turn would have less to spend on cloth, labor, and other inputs, so we should expect to see lower price levels in those sectors of the economy. The higher prices in one sector would be offset by lower prices in other sectors, as long as there is only so much money to go around.

Recessions Do Not Lower Inflation

Samuelson also says that "downturns check inflation." But that ain't so either, at least not when we consider what happens after the recession. He says, plausibly, that "it's harder to increase wages and prices" in a downturn. While this may be true during the downturn, if the money supply is increasing unabated—so that eventually prices and wages will have to adjust to the larger money supply—people's hesitancy to raise wages and prices during the downturn simply creates a lag. Prices and wages will have to catch up later.

In practice, causation will more frequently run the other way, with inflation today causing a downturn later. As Steven Horwitz and others have explained, inflation not only increases the level of prices, it also distorts relative prices, the economy's essential means of communicating the relative scarcity of various goods, and thereby interferes with economic coordination. That interference can itself cause or prolong recessions. The longest period of poor economic performance in my lifetime was the 1970s, a period of inflationary recession. Not only did the long, deep downturns of that decade not "check inflation," on the contrary the inflation likely deepened the downturns.

Friedman's maxim bears frequent repeating. Who controls the money supply controls inflation. As for any claim to the contrary, it just ain't so.

*"What we will have for the next 30
years is inflation."*

Rising Wages Cause Inflation

Shai Oster

*Shai Oster is a US journalist based in Hong Kong. In the following
viewpoint, he says that the Chinese workforce is shrinking, and the
Chinese are attempting to improve working conditions. As a result,
Oster says, labor costs in China will rise steeply, which means that
the cost of goods will go up. Oster says this will have a major impact on prices in the West, where consumer good costs have been
held down by the low cost of Chinese labor. Oster concludes that
inflation, which has been low for decades in the West, is likely to
begin to accelerate.*

As you read, consider the following questions:

1. By how much does William Fung predict that wages in
   China will increase over the next five years?
2. What is Foxconn and why did it raise wages, according to
   Oster?
3. Where in China does Oster say that labor is still cheap?

Wages are rising in China, heralding the possible end of an era of cheap goods.

Wages and Prices Are Rising

For the past 30 years, customers would ask William Fung, the managing director of one of the world's biggest manufacturing-outsourcing companies, to make his products—whether T-shirts, jeans or dishes—cheaper. Thanks to China's seemingly limitless labor force, he usually could.

Now, the head of Li & Fung Ltd. says the times are changing. Wages for the tens of thousands of workers his Hong Kong-based firm indirectly employs are surging: He predicts overall, China's wages will increase 80% over the next five years. That means prices for Li & Fung's goods will have to rise, too.

"What we will have for the next 30 years is inflation," Mr. Fung said. "A lot of Western managers have never coped with inflation."

The issue is likely to hover behind talks Monday [May 2011], between Chinese and U.S. leaders in Washington at their annual Strategic Economic Dialogue. Currency and debt issues are expected to dominate the agenda. But there are signs that the low labor costs—and cheap currency—that led to China's huge trade surplus with the U.S. could be reaching a tipping point. This comes amid pressure from rising wages as China's working-age population begins to decline.

For decades, plentiful Chinese labor kept down costs of a range of goods bought by Americans. Even as politicians in Washington accused China of hollowing out the American manufacturing sector, cheap DVD players, sweaters and barbecue sets were a silver lining for consumers who grew accustomed to ever-lower prices. China also kept down the value of its currency, giving domestic exporters a competitive edge.

"Inflation has been damped pretty dramatically in the U.S. because it exported work to China and other places at 20% or 30% of the cost," said Hal Sirkin, a consultant at Boston Consulting Group. The years of dramatic reductions in costs are over, the firm says.

The Foxconn Effect

Li & Fung traces the start of rising wages to the "Foxconn Effect." Foxconn is the trade name of Hon Hai Precision Industry Co., maker of iPads for Apple Inc., and computers for Hewlett-Packard Co., among others. After a string of worker suicides last year at one of its China plants spurred Foxconn to defend its treatment of employees, the company raised wages 30% or more in a bid to improve worker conditions. That raise came as workers at other factories, including staff at a Honda Motor Co. parts plant, went on strike for higher pay.

Since then, the Chinese government has supported higher wages in part to address labor unrest, but also as [a] way to boost domestic consumption and reduce reliance on exports to expand the economy. The rising wages affect both foreign and domestic companies.

Other factors besides rising wages are pushing up the price of goods. Chinese workers, for one, are starting to buy more with their higher salaries. That's contributing to higher prices for commodities such as cotton and oil, which are already climbing in part because of a weaker dollar. Rising living standards in developing economies like China will keep prices of natural resources high as demand outpaces supply.

China's move to let the yuan [the Chinese currency] slowly appreciate in value—something eagerly sought by its Western trading partners—adds fuel to the fire. A stronger yuan makes it cheaper for China to import the raw materials it needs, such as iron and soybeans, helping tame domestic inflation. But it makes its exported goods more expensive for other countries to buy.

"This idea that we have moved from an era of easy deflationary environment to one of inflation is correct," said Jeffrey Sachs, economist and director of the Earth Institute at Columbia University.

During China's 30 years of economic growth, hundreds of millions of factory and urban jobs soaked up surplus rural farm

HOLLYWOOD TALENT

"SORRY, KID, BUT THERE'S A DOG IN CHINA WHO WILL BARK 'JUNGLE BELLS' FOR A THIRD WHAT WE PAY YOU!"

Cartoon by Jack Corbett. www.CartoonStock.com.

labor. In the past three or four years, he says, that extra labor has been exhausted.

Labor Force Decline

Many analysts predict that China's vast labor force will begin declining in the next year or two, the result of family-planning policies.[1] Others say there's already a shortage of the most active members of the factory floor, workers aged 15 to 34. That group has been steadily declining since 2007, according to Jun Ma, Deutsche Bank's chief economist for Greater China. A shrinking work force will need higher salaries to support an expanding population of elderly.

There's some debate about the impact and extent of these wage increases on foreign markets. The pace of inflation for U.S. imports is running around 7% this year, but it doesn't account for a big enough portion of spending to significantly affect overall low inflation rates of about 1.6%, Morgan Stanley's China strategist Jonathan Garner said. Still, with real wages stagnant for decades, many Americans who have grown dependent on cheap imported goods such as polo shirts or power tools could see their purchasing power decrease.

China still has cheap labor in its interior, away from its developed coastal cities, and productivity gains could mitigate higher wage costs. For example, Foxconn announced it was expanding operations to inland areas near Chengdu, Wuhan, and Zhengzhou, away from its coastal base. Li & Fung is encouraging its suppliers to invest more in their factories to increase worker productivity and raise the quality of goods.

There are limits to what those measures will achieve. Some analysts say that the wage increases will sharply outpace any productivity gains. Moving inland means lower wages, but higher transportation costs on China's crowded highways and railroads. Furthermore, locating the factories in China's hinterland puts them in a better position to service China's growing domestic consumer market instead of exporting to consumers in the U.S. and elsewhere.

Faced with rising wages within China, some companies are shifting resources elsewhere to keep costs down. Yue Yuen Industrial (Holdings) Ltd., the world's biggest shoe maker, has started moving manufacturing of low-cost shoes from China to countries such as Bangladesh and Cambodia. Li & Fung has . . . hired a prominent Chinese sneaker brand, Li Ning Co., to help it search for cheap production outside China.

But the wage gap between China and other developing countries will shrink, said Mr. Fung, echoing views shared by Boston Consulting Group, because "China was the thing that kept the price low," he says. "China was the benchmark. With the China price rising, everyone else wants to raise prices."

As factories relocate to other countries, local wages will rise faster than they did in China because the potential pools of surplus labor are smaller. In addition, because no other country can replicate the massive scale of China, logistics will become a larger part of costs as companies are forced to slice up their manufacturing over several countries, analysts say.

"Things will be more expensive and people will buy less," Mr. Fung warns. That means that the West will have to adopt new consumption trends.

Note

1. China's one-child policy limits each family to one child except under special circumstances.

| "Unions . . . cannot change the supply of money. If their actions do not somehow indirectly alter the demand for money, then they clearly cannot change the price of money."

Unions and Rising Wages Do Not Cause Inflation

Robert P. Murphy

Robert P. Murphy is an adjunct scholar at the Ludwig Von Mises Institute and author of The Politically Incorrect Guide to Capitalism. *In the following viewpoint, he argues that unions are not responsible for inflation. Murphy says that prices only rise when there is an increase in the money supply. Unions cannot increase the money supply. Therefore, he says, unions can cause inefficiencies and distortions in the economy, but they cannot cause inflation. Murphy concludes that only a central bank can increase inflation by increasing the money supply.*

As you read, consider the following questions:
1. How does Murphy define the price of money?
2. What determines the price of money, according to Murphy?

3. What does Murphy say has to "give" if wages in a particular sector rise and the money supply remains the same?

Central banks around the world have painted themselves into a corner as of late, as their plans for injecting hundreds of billions of dollars worth of credit into the financial markets butts up against their desire to avoid massive price increases. Rather than take the blame for this predicament, the financial central planners have characteristically started pointing fingers elsewhere. In the January 5–6 [2008] weekend edition of the *Wall Street Journal*, we learn that it is apparently unions who are now at fault:

> European trade unions are preparing aggressive pay demands for 2008. . . . This is sure to grate on [European Central Bank] President Jean-Claude Trichet, who has been escalating his warnings that a wage-driven boost in euro-zone inflation would provoke an increase in official interest rates. The ECB calls it "second-round" inflation effect, which essentially doubles existing inflation as workers demand higher wages and companies pass on higher costs to customers.

In the present [viewpoint] we'll try to sort these complicated issues out, but first we need a quick primer on monetary theory. Now I warn you, the following section will be more difficult to digest than an episode of the *Colbert Report*, [a satirical television show] but we'll make it as painless as possible. On the bright side, the reader's thinking on inflation will be much clearer when it's done.

The Price of Money

The "price" of money is how many units of goods and services a person needs to give up, in order to acquire a unit of money. It is the reciprocal of what we normally think of as prices (quoted in money). For example, if a car is $5,000, then one dollar has a "price" of 1/5,000 of a car. Or, if a gumball is 25 cents, then one dollar has a price of four gumballs.

It sounds funny to talk like this, but the oddity reflects the great service that money performs: by always constituting one side of every transaction, the money good allows us to think of "the" price of everything else merely in terms of its money exchange rate. If there were no single item that everyone traded against—in other words, if every seller didn't first acquire money before seeking out the things he or she ultimately desired—then there would be no single exchange rate that everyone would agree on, when quoting prices. People who really cared about gumballs might go around, thinking, "That item's worth 42 gumballs. That massage would cost me 3000 gumballs" and so forth, while somebody else might view the economy in terms of cars.

Unfortunately, we can't use the convenience of a single number for the "price" of money, simply because this is the one good it would be silly to price in terms of money. We learn something about the state of the economy when we know that a car has a price of $5,000, while a gumball has a price of 25 cents (i.e., 0.25 dollars). But it doesn't really tell us anything if we say that one dollar has a price of one dollar, even though that's a true statement.

The price of money, therefore, can be quoted as any of the millions of possible exchange rates with other items in the economy. Generally speaking, the price of money is its *purchasing power,* which is the inverse of what people mean by "the price level," although that's a very sloppy term. It would be less misleading to speak of the price *array* or price *constellation.* The popular term price *level* is misleading because we can express the purchasing power of money only by listing the millions of exchange rates it has against every good and service in the economy, and there is no reason for this list of numbers to change uniformly over time.

So we see that money has a price, just like other goods, but that expressing the price is a bit uncomfortable, precisely because it is money that makes it a snap to express the price of every *other* good (and service) in the economy. To put it in other words, it's not that it's *difficult* to express the price of money—rather it's that money itself makes it *easy* to express the prices of all nonmoney items.

Price Set by Supply and Demand

As with everything else, the price of money is determined by supply and demand. The supply side is easy enough; at any moment, there is a definite amount of dollars—both in people's wallets and also their checking account balances—in the world. . . .

But what of the demand side? Can economists analyze the "demand for money" the same way they look at the demand for plasma screen TVs?

The answer is yes, but we first need to be clear about a common confusion. When it comes to money, the beginner should think in terms of *stocks*, not flows. At any point in time, every single dollar bill is owned by someone, and is part of someone's cash balance. There is no such thing as money "in circulation," to be contrasted with "hoarded" money. *All* money is being hoarded, in the sense that every last dollar bill is always being held by someone who—at that precise moment—considers it more advantageous to hold the marginal unit of money, rather than to exchange it for something else. (Of course, many dollar bills are being held in the cash balances of the owners of grocery stores and banks, and are sitting in the tills of their establishments. But this money too is part of cash balances; it's not "in circulation.")

In theory, there are all sorts of reasons that people might desire to hold cash balances. There might be people who adore the US presidency, for example, and can't believe how little they have to work in order to acquire yet another wallet-sized portrait of those handsome gents.

However, the main element constituting the demand for cash balances is the expectation of its purchasing power in the future. Strange as it seems, the cash sitting in your wallet or purse performs a service just by sitting there. It reassures you, in the same way that having a fire extinguisher under your kitchen sink reassures you.

Let's think about this a little more. If your teenage son came home from Sam's Club with six years' worth of bottled water, and proudly explained that he had emptied out the family checking account because there was "such a good deal," this would be incredibly stressful. And note that the precise reason for your anger would *not* be whether or not your son overpaid for the water, but rather that he drew down your cash balance and invested it in goods that were far less liquid (in the economic, not physical sense!) than cash.

At any given time, people want to hold a certain amount of *purchasing power* in the form of liquid cash (or completely trustworthy checkbook deposits). This desire constitutes the demand for money, and interacts with the supply of money to yield the price of money at that moment. In equilibrium, the available stock of money is distributed into all of the cash holdings of everyone in the economy, and all of the money prices of the various goods and services are at just the right amounts, so that each person is holding the desired amount of purchasing power.

Before leaving this section, let's go over a popular thought experiment to make sure we understand how to use this framework we've developed. Suppose one day that a helicopter drops extra dollar bills into everyone's backyard. What will happen?

The first, immediate effect will be that everyone who picks up the new money will have a higher cash balance (both in terms of absolute dollars and in purchasing power) than before. Let's suppose for simplicity that everyone originally had $1,000 in cash, and now the helicopter has doubled everyone's cash balance to $2,000. If the prices (quoted in dollars) of goods and services don't adjust, then people will be holding more purchasing power than they want to maintain. To be sure, people may always want more *wealth*, but they don't necessarily want to hold it in ever-larger stockpiles of *cash*.

If the demand for cash remains the same, then the only way to restore equilibrium is for the (money) prices of goods and services to rise. If we simplistically assume away all the real world complications of timing and so forth, we can imagine that the dollar price for every good and service in the economy doubles, as people rush out to spend some of their newly found money. Then things are back to how they were before the helicopter drop. People now hold $2,000 in their cash balances, but because prices have doubled, this represents the same purchasing power as it did before. The injection of new money hasn't created any real wealth, it has simply caused prices to rise. (And again, we are ignoring all of the distortions due to the adjustment phase.)

For those who like to think in terms of the dreaded graphs of undergraduate economics, what happened in the helicopter example is that the supply of money increased, while the demand for money stayed the same. This means that the price of money had to fall, i.e., the dollar prices of goods and services had to rise, making a particular unit of money less valuable relative to other items.

Can Unions Cause Price Inflation?

We can now return to the original issue: if union agitation leads to wage increases, will that cause prices in general to increase?

The quick answer is, "No, not if the demand for money remains the same." If unions succeed in wage hikes, and employers raise the prices they charge consumers to maintain their own profit margins, *and the supply of money remains the same*, then something else has to "give." Either the prices of goods and services in nonunion sectors have to fall and offset the union sector hikes, or people's cash balances need to fall, in terms of their purchasing power.

Remember, it is a mistake to think that the workers are sucking money out of the economy; the workers *are* a large portion of the consumers, after all. Rather, if the number of dollar bills remains constant, while prices in general go up, then cash balances (measured in purchasing power) must fall. This could be true even for the workers who achieved large pay hikes. They might consider their financial position superior to their previous one, but even so the amount of cash in their wallets and checking accounts could be uncomfortably low compared to the higher prices of the goods and services they want to buy in the coming weeks and months.

As we said above, if the demand for cash balances remains the same, then this situation cannot last. People are not holding enough purchasing power, and so they restrict their purchases in order to build up a larger stockpile of liquid funds. Merchants will experience a decline in sales, and will have to slash prices if they want to stay in business.

To repeat our conclusion: unions . . . cannot change the supply of money. If their actions do not somehow indirectly alter the demand for money, then they clearly cannot change the price of money. In other words, unions can't directly cause price inflation. By distorting *relative* prices and insisting on inefficient workplace rules, they certainly hamper the economy, no question about it. But it is wrong to blame unions for rising prices.

Central Bankers, Not Unions, Cause Inflation

In closing, I should acknowledge that there is a way for the European Central Bank story to work. The above framework doesn't rule out the theoretical possibility that union agitation leads to wage hikes, which in turn lead to general price hikes, and that a resigned populace shrugs its shoulders and accepts the lower purchasing power of its cash holdings.

However, I think in practice the population will react by "spreading the pain." Rather than directing the hit fully into depreciated cash holdings, people will cut back on their discretionary purchases. This greatly mutes the alleged power of the unions to raise prices *in general*, especially if the initial wage hikes are limited to a few industries.

No, when it comes to the reasons for rising prices—especially as this price inflation occurs year in, year out—the true culprit seems clear enough: it is the central bankers who continually add new dollars (and euros, etc.) to their respective economies. Rather than worrying about union-inspired "second-round" inflation, the ECB should focus on its own *first*-round inflation.

> "Investors were generally pleased with
> the latest [2005] GDP data. . . . [Their]
> enthusiasm was muted somewhat by
> concerns [about] . . . interest rate hikes
> from the Federal Reserve to combat
> inflation."

Stocks Move Higher on Strong GDP Report

Michael J. Martinez

*Michael J. Martinez is the Business writer for the Associated Press.
In the following viewpoint, he claims that there are concerns that
economic growth and growth in GDP will cause a rise in inflation and interest. The GDP growth in 2005, noted in the article,
helped the dollar gain ground against the euro. The main concern
of Wall Street and the public alike is the rise in interest rates from
the Federal Reserve as they try to combat inflation.*

As you read, consider the following questions:

1. As stated in the article, by what was Wall Street's enthusiasm muted?
2. According to the viewpoint, did the GDP help the dollar
   gain ground against the euro?

3. How much was a barrel of light crude at the time the article was written?

Stronger-than-expected growth in the nation's gross domestic product pushed stocks higher Friday as investors weighed the benefits of an improving economy against the possibility of higher inflation.

Investors were generally pleased with the latest GDP data, which showed the economy growing at an annualized rate of 3.8 percent in the fourth quarter, up from last month's 3.1 percent estimate from the Commerce Department and better than economists' 3.5 percent forecast.

However, Wall Street's enthusiasm was muted somewhat by concerns that stronger economic growth would lead to faster and more aggressive interest rate hikes from the Federal Reserve to combat inflation.

In late morning trading, the Dow Jones industrial average rose 30.97, or 0.3 percent, to 10,779.76.

Broader stock indicators were modestly higher. The Standard & Poor's 500 index was up 4.96, or 0.4 percent, at 1,205.16, and the technology-focused Nasdaq composite index gained 4.50, or 0.2 percent, to 2,056.20.

The GDP helped the dollar gain ground against the euro for the first time this week, though the dollar remained mixed against other currencies. The bond market was mostly unchanged on the news, with the yield on the 10-year Treasury note holding at 4.29 percent.

Crude oil futures—which rose substantially earlier this week as the dollar tumbled—fell slightly after the GDP report. A barrel of light crude was quoted at $51.23, down 16 cents, on the New York Mercantile Exchange.

Oil stocks rallied as priced started to climb, resuming their place at the forefront of the market. Exxon Mobil Corp. was up $1.72 at $62.85, while ChevronTexaco Corp. added $1.67 to $62.83 and ConocoPhilips climbed $2.72 to $112.90.

When Unemployment Goes Up, Inflation Goes Down

In a celebrated article published in 1958, Australian economist A.W. Phillips of the London School of Economics plotted data on unemployment rates and the rate of change in wage rates between 1861 and 1957 in the United Kingdom. Phillips showed there was a remarkably stable inverse relationship [when one went up the other went down] between changes in money wages and the unemployment rate. Economists have since extended this concept to the following definition of the Phillips curve. The Phillips curve is a curve showing an inverse relationship between the inflation rate and the unemployment rate. The reason it is acceptable to use the inflation rate, rather than the change in wages, is that wages are the main component of prices. At low rates of unemployment, labor has the market power to push up wages and, in turn, prices. When many workers are pounding the pavement eager for jobs, labor lacks bargaining power to ask for raises. As a result, the upward pressure on prices eases.

Irvin B. Tucker, Macroeconomics for Today. *Mason, OH: South-Western Cengage Learning, 2011, p. 453.*

"You've seen energy stocks taking off while technology stocks have been lagging since mid-December," said Ken Tower, chief market strategist for Schwab's CyberTrader. "I think if energy stocks are going to lead the market, then tech stocks won't be. Energy stocks represent higher consumer prices, and that will cause technology stocks to suffer."

Qwest Communications International Inc. fell 21 cents to $3.99 after it improved its $8 billion offer for MCI Inc., adding a provision to guarantee the stock portion of its bid. Dow component Verizon Communications Inc., which already had its $6.7 billion offer for MCI accepted last week, climbed 41 cents to $35.91.

MCI lost 32 cents to $22.49 after reporting a loss of 10 cents per share for the fourth quarter. Excluding one-time charges, however, the company beat Wall Street's profit and revenue forecasts.

The Wall Street Journal reported Friday that the boards of directors for Federated Department Stores Inc. and May Department Stores Co. would meet in the next few days to finalize Federated's bid for its struggling rival, valued at more than $10 billion. Federated fell 57 cents to $56.44, while May rose $1.03 to $34.88.

In earnings news, The Gap Inc. added 31 cents to $21.59 after the clothing retailer beat Wall Street's fourth-quarter profit expectations by 3 cents per share. The company said it would also double its annual dividend.

Department store chain Kohl's Corp. beat analysts' forecasts by a penny per share in the fourth quarter, crediting stronger sales and higher margins. Kohl's gained $1.85 to $47.75.

Advancing issues outnumbered decliners by nearly 7 to 5 on the New York Stock Exchange, where volume came to 390.78 million shares, compared with 429.97 million at the same point on Thursday.

The Russell 2000 index of smaller companies was up 3.25, or 0.5 percent, at 630.81.

Overseas, Japan's Nikkei stock average rose 1.1 percent. In afternoon trading, Britain's FTSE 100 was up 0.4 percent, Germany's DAX index gained 0.84 percent, and France's CAC-40 climbed 1.01 percent.

> *"If something doesn't cause the money used within the economy to become worth less, then the production of more 'stuff' will result in LOWER prices for the 'stuff.'"*

Economic Growth Does Not Cause Inflation

Steve Saville

Steve Saville is the editor of the Speculative Investor. *In the following viewpoint he argues that economic growth does not cause inflation. He says that if the economy grows and more things are produced, this should drive prices down. He argues that central banks claim growth causes inflation to cover up the fact that central banks are the ones causing inflation. He says inflation only occurs when central banks increase the money supply.*

As you read, consider the following questions:

1. Why does Saville believe that central bankers have an excuse for spreading misinformation?
2. How does Saville define the term "velocity of money"?
3. According to Saville, why does the demand for money fall?

W e often read about the inflation threat posed by stronger economic growth, with the word inflation here referring to a rise in the general price level. Inflation is, of course, a rise in the total supply of money, but for the purposes of this discussion there's no need to dwell on the importance of getting this particular definition right. What we'll dwell on today is the absurdity of the notion that growth causes prices to rise.

More Stuff, Lower Prices

Central bankers will regularly refer to something called "the rate of economic growth consistent with low inflation" as if a higher rate of real economic growth would be expected to lead to troublesome increases in the general price level. The implication is that inflation occurs because the economy, for some unspecified reason, begins to charge ahead at an excessive speed, and that when this happens it falls upon the central bank to do something to solve the problem.

Central bankers, however, have an excuse for spreading misinformation because one of their primary job requirements is to deceive. In order to maintain confidence in the monetary system the central bank must be vigilant in its efforts to direct attention away from the true source of the inflation (the central bank itself) and towards things that don't cast aspersions on the nature of today's national currencies. In this respect, 'too strong' economic growth is just a convenient excuse for a general rise in the price level, as are, from time to time, things such as oil supply shocks, the weather, increased Chinese consumption of commodities and the wage-hike demands of labour unions.

But what excuse do independent analysts/economists (those whose work is not funded by the government) have for spreading the lie that growth is somehow responsible for economy-wide increases in prices? That it is a lie will be immediately apparent to anyone who asks themselves the simple question: "How could the production of MORE goods and services possibly do anything other than put DOWNWARD pressure on the general price level?"

If something doesn't cause the money used within the economy to become worth less, then the production of more 'stuff' will result in LOWER prices for the 'stuff'. Therefore, when more stuff is produced and prices still rise we know, for certain, that something MUST be causing money to lose its purchasing power at a fast enough rate to more than offset the positive effects, on the money's purchasing power, of the real growth. What is happening, in this case, is that the supply of money is increasing relative to the demand for money.

Concealing the Truth

But couldn't an increase in the "velocity of money" (the rate at which the same money gets passed from person to person within an economy) cause the general price level to rise even if the supply of money remained constant?

The answer is no. Even if "velocity" were a useful monetary concept (it isn't) an increase in the velocity of money would have to be caused by something; the velocity of money couldn't just increase for no reason. So, someone who argued that an increase in the velocity of money was causing an increase in the general price level would then have to explain what was causing the increase in velocity in the first place.

"Money velocity" is a concept that is meaningless at best and dangerous at worst. It is potentially dangerous because, like the whole "growth causes inflation" argument, it helps to conceal the truth about what causes money to lose purchasing power. If, for example, the economy-wide demand for money begins to fall then people will be quicker to exchange their money for the things that money can buy and economists will observe an increase in the velocity of money. However, the crux of the matter is the reason WHY the demand for money is falling. The economy-wide demand for money doesn't fall in response to people becoming more productive; it falls because people expect the money to be worth less in the future than it is today.

In a growing economy, the ONLY way the general price level can rise over a long period of time is via an increase in the supply of money. Furthermore, under the current monetary system it is the central bank that ultimately controls how much new money is created. That is, the central bank causes inflation.

| "Monetary policy also has an important influence on inflation."

The Federal Reserve Influences Inflation Through Monetary Policy

Board of Governors of the Federal Reserve System

The Federal Reserve System is the central bank of the United States. In the following viewpoint, the authors explain that the Federal Reserve (commonly known as "the Fed") buys securities to inject money into the economy and lower interest rates (which is the cost of borrowing). The Fed says that lowering interest rates can encourage people to borrow and invest, which stimulates the economy. However, lowering interest rates increases demand, which can increase inflation. This can hurt the economy. The Fed tries to balance interest rates to encourage growth without creating too much inflation.

As you read, consider the following questions:

1. As stated in the article, when are households more willing to buy goods?

2. Why is it difficult to gauge the effect of monetary policy?
3. What happens when the federal funds rate is reduced as stated in the viewpoint?

In the short run, monetary policy influences inflation and the economy-wide demand for goods and services—and, therefore, the demand for the employees who produce those goods and services—primarily through its influence on the financial conditions facing households and firms. During normal times, the Federal Reserve has primarily influenced overall financial conditions by adjusting the federal funds rate—the rate that banks charge each other for short-term loans. Movements in the federal funds rate are passed on to other short-term interest rates that influence borrowing costs for firms and households. Movements in short-term interest rates also influence long-term interest rates—such as corporate bond rates and residential mortgage rates—because those rates reflect, among other factors, the current and expected future values of short-term rates. In addition, shifts in long-term interest rates affect other asset prices, most notably equity prices and the foreign exchange value of the dollar. For example, all else being equal, lower interest rates tend to raise equity prices as investors discount the future cash flows associated with equity investments at a lower rate.

Change in Financial Conditions and Economic Activity

In turn, these changes in financial conditions affect economic activity. For example, when short- and long-term interest rates go down, it becomes cheaper to borrow, so households are more willing to buy goods and services and firms are in a better position to purchase items to expand their businesses, such as property and equipment. Firms respond to these increases in total (household and business) spending by hiring more workers and boosting production. As a result of these factors, household wealth increases, which spurs even more spending. These linkages from monetary policy to production and employment don't show up immediately and are influenced by a range of factors, which makes it difficult to gauge precisely the effect of monetary policy on the economy.

Monetary policy also has an important influence on inflation. When the federal funds rate is reduced, the resulting stronger demand for goods and services tends to push wages and other costs higher, reflecting the greater demand for workers and materials that are necessary for production. In addition, policy actions can influence expectations about how the economy will perform in the future, including expectations for prices and wages, and those expectations can themselves directly influence current inflation.

At the end of 2008, with short-term interest rates essentially at zero and thus unable to fall much further, the Federal Reserve undertook unconventional monetary policy measures to provide additional support to the economy. So, the Federal Reserve purchased longer-term mortgage-backed securities and notes issued by certain government-sponsored enterprises, as well as longer-term Treasury bonds and notes. The primary purpose of the program was to try to lower the level of longer-term interest rates, thereby improving financial conditions. Thus, this unconventional monetary policy operates through the same broad channels as conventional policy, despite the differences in implementation of the policy.

> "Monetary policy is far too blunt a tool
> for encouraging the type of targeted
> and carefully calibrated price increases
> that Fed officials want."

The Federal Reserve Cannot Control Inflation

John Kemp

John Kemp is a financial columnist for Reuters *specializing in commodities and energy markets. In the following viewpoint he argues that there is no single rate of inflation in the economy. Instead, he says, different goods have prices that rise and fall at different rates. As a result, he says, the Federal Reserve's efforts to spur inflation and growth will have unexpected consequences. If the Fed tries to stimulate housing markets for example, it will spur inflation in energy and food sectors, Kemp says. He concludes that the Fed should think twice before trying to cause inflation.*

As you read, consider the following questions:

1. What prices does Kemp say are rising quickly and which items in the United States have prices that are rising more slowly?

2. According to Kemp, policymakers in the United States have identified inflation with what different measures?
3. What has been the inflation trend for shelter over the last two decades, according to Kemp?

In 1987, UK Prime Minister Margaret Thatcher whipped up a firestorm of criticism from her opponents on the left when she told a magazine reporter that "there is no such thing as society", only individual men and women, and families.

The interpretation of those comments remains fiercely controversial. From the context it is not certain the prime minister was clear what she was trying to say.

But according to one interpretation the prime minister was encouraging her listeners to look beyond the impersonal aggregate of "society" to the individuals behind it.

No Such Thing as Inflation

The distinction between aggregates and individual components is something the Federal Reserve [the US Central bank] should bear in mind as officials mull whether to launch a new round of asset purchases to keep inflation from falling further and stimulate the recovery.

Because in some sense there is no such thing as inflation, only a collection of price rises for individual items, some rising faster and some slower.

It is clear price increases do have a structural component. Policymakers and economists distinguish between a general rise in the level of prices ("inflation") and relative price increases for individual items (Adam Smith's "invisible hand"[1] guiding the reallocation of scarce resources).

But in an economy characterized by uneven spare capacity, with bottlenecks in some areas and unused capacity in others, excess demand and inflationary pressures may not show up evenly. Even as all prices rise (inflation), price rises are likely to be largest in those parts of the system with the worst bottlenecks, while increases in areas suffering significant under-employment of resources lag behind.

The problem for the Fed is that the prices of some items that are in relatively short supply internationally (iron ore, oil, foodstuffs, cotton) are rising quickly while other items where there is a local surplus (U.S. housing, U.S. manufacturing and U.S. wages) are rising more slowly. There is no guarantee adding more liquidity [more money] to the economy will close the gap or even affect all prices equally.

By the time the Fed has added enough liquidity to overcome structural problems and stimulate a modest rise in U.S. house prices, manufacturing prices and wages, it will probably have caused a conflagration in oil, metals, grains and other internationally traded commodities. Monetary policy is far too blunt a tool for encouraging the type of targeted and carefully calibrated price increases that Fed officials want.

Not One Rate but Many

Focusing on the "average" rate of price increases is apt to mislead. There is not one single rate of inflation but a whole family of them:

1. In the United States, policymakers have at different times identified "inflation" with the consumer price index for all urban consumers (CPI-U); the consumer price index excluding food and energy items (core CPI-U); the GDP deflator for personal consumption expenditures (PCE); and the market-based personal expenditures deflator excluding food and energy. The inflation rates given by these measures can and have been utterly different. They don't even necessarily move in the same direction.

2. In the United Kingdom, inflation rates given by the retail prices index (RPI) and consumer price index (CPI) have been so different in recent years that the government is

shifting indexation of at least some parts of the budget from the (higher) RPI to the (lower) CPI in a bid to cut costs.

3. In response to popular and media complaints that published inflation rates are not consistent with households' own experience of rising prices, and generally understate the rate of increase, statisticians across North America and Europe have pointed out that:

a. Published inflation rates are averages—individual households may have higher or lower personal rates depending on the basket of goods and services they buy.

b. Personal impressions are skewed when prices for low-value frequently bought items (food and fuel) are rising rapidly while more expensive but less frequently purchased items (consumer electronics and durables) are rising more slowly or even falling.

Inflation rates and price indexes are useful short-hand ways to think about the rate of change in a broad basket of prices. But they are a very imperfect reflection of the "cost of living" let alone trying to fine tune the economy. Every person reading this [viewpoint] will have their own experience of "inflation".

The problem for the Fed is that different components of the consumer price index are diverging and there is no easy way to stimulate increases in housing, manufactured items and wages without triggering an even more rapid escalation in the cost of energy and food (which could cut spending further since these are costs for most households and corporations).

[The graph shows] the 12-month increase in the three major components of the U.S. consumer price index—food and energy; shelter (owners' equivalent rent); and other items. Food/energy and shelter each account for about a quarter of the total weighting, other items account for just under half.

Food and energy have been much more volatile that the rest of the index and have become increasingly unstable in recent

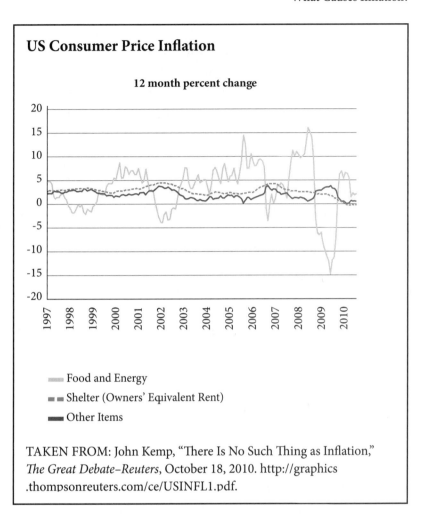

US Consumer Price Inflation

12 month percent change

— Food and Energy

– – Shelter (Owners' Eqivalent Rent)

— Other Items

TAKEN FROM: John Kemp, "There Is No Such Thing as Inflation," *The Great Debate–Reuters*, October 18, 2010. http://graphics .thompsonreuters.com/ce/USINFL1.pdf.

years. Inflation in shelter and other items has been much more stable and gently trending downwards for the last two decades.

The Fed's problem is that while food and energy prices are still rising briskly (2.16 percent in the twelve months to September), other items barely increased (up 0.47 percent) and the cost of shelter as measured by owners' equivalent rent actually fell (down −0.10 percent).

This is not the first time inflation in the "other items" category has fallen very low. But in 2003 and again in 2005–2006, ultra-low inflation for other items was offset by faster increases in shelter and food/energy. This time shelter costs are falling and food/energy costs are going up only relatively slowly.

The pattern of price rises looks structural rather than cyclical. Inflation in shelter and other items has been on a downtrend for 20 years due to globalisation, off-shoring, better supply chain management, and better wage control, all of which are due to secular trends rather than a short term loss of demand. The sudden disappearance of inflation in the shelter sector is the legacy of the housing bust.[2] Much of the current low inflation problem looks like a simple after-effect of the housing crash.

Both the shelter and the other items components of the CPI have been remarkably stable over the last two decades. To generate an appreciable increase in these two components of the CPI which account for 25 percent and 50 percent of the index respectively, the Fed would probably need to apply an enormous amount of stimulus, buying hundreds of billions if not trillions of financial assets.

Stability and Instability

The food/energy component in contrast is much more unstable. Because these markets have much less spare capacity, inflation rates have remained higher. If the Fed applied enough stimulus to lift shelter and other items appreciably, it would probably cause a huge increase in the food/energy component as well as an enormous bubble in asset prices such as bonds and equities.

The same problem is being replicated within the energy/food complex itself. Prospective quantitative easing[3] is already causing prices for commodities thought to be in short supply (gold, grains, copper and cotton) to rise much faster than those with spare capacity and slack fundamentals (crude oil and natural gas).

Before they launch a massive asset purchase programme, Fed officials need to ask precisely what sort of inflation they are trying to stimulate, and how QE [quantitative easing] will achieve it without triggering lots of unintended and harmful side effects.

Notes

1. Adam Smith was a major economist in the 1700s. The "invisible hand" is the idea that individuals acting on their own self-interest without direction create social benefits.
2. In 2008, housing prices in the United States plummeted, contributing to a major worldwide financial crisis.
3. Quantitative easing is a technique the Fed uses to increase money supply.

Periodical and Internet Sources Bibliography

The following articles have been selected to supplement the diverse views presented in this chapter.

Tania Branigan	"China's Growth Fuels Overheating Fears," *Guardian*, January 20, 2011. www.guardian.co.uk.
Wang Guanyi	"Lower GDP Growth Rate Is Beneficial to Economy," *ChinaDaily*, March 11, 2011. usa.chinadaily.com.cn
John T. Harvey	"Money Growth Does Not Cause Inflation!" *Forbes*, May 14, 2011. www.forbes.com.
Owen Humpage	"Can the Federal Reserve Control Inflation in a Global Marketplace?," *Forefront*, Spring 2011. www.clevelandfed.org.
ICS Trust	"Wage Increases in China Will Push Inflation," March 23, 2011. www.icstrust.com.
Linette Lopez	"China Just Issued a Warning to Anyone Worried About Inflation," *Business Insider*, June 29, 2011. articles.businessinsider.com.
Nancy Marshall-Genzer	"Is There a Way to Control Inflation?," *Marketplace*, January 13, 2011. www.marketplace.org.
Felix Salmon	"Should the Fed Be Worried About Wage Inflation?," Reuters, May 19, 2011. http://blogs.reuters.com.
Shad Satterthwaite	"What Is the Federal Reserve and What Does It Do?," ThisNation.com. http://thisnation.com.
Frank Shostak	"Does Economic Growth Cause Inflation?" Ludwig von Mises Institute, March 16, 2011. http://mises.org.
John Tamny	"Growth Does Not Cause Inflation," *Forbes*, June 8, 2009. http://www.forbes.com.

OPPOSING
VIEWPOINTS®
SERIES

Chapter 2

Is Inflation Dangerous?

Chapter Preface

Following the financial crisis of 2008, many homeowners saw the prices of their homes drop steeply. As a result, many people found that they owed more on their mortgages than their homes were worth. Their homes were said to be "underwater." Owners could no longer sell their properties for enough to pay off the cost of the home. Because paying into the home was essentially a loss, and owners couldn't sell the homes anyway, they were likely to stop paying, default, and let the house revert to the bank.

Some experts argue that an increase in inflation would provide relief to many of those with underwater mortgages, which would in turn help revitalize the economy. Dean Baker argues in an October 7, 2011, article for the Center for Economic and Policy Research that a higher rate of inflation would raise home prices and pull many homes out from underwater. Baker says:

"Just to throw out some simple numbers, suppose the Fed targeted a 5–6 percent inflation rate over the next two years . . . if we assume that house prices rise more or less in step with inflation, then many currently underwater homeowners will come back up above water. Someone who owes $220,000 on a house that is today worth $200,000 will likely be back above water again in two years."

Baker notes that the policy will not just benefit underwater homeowners. With inflation, everybody's home price would rise, even those who are not distressed.

Though inflation might help debtors, inflationary policies can harm other parts of the economy. Claes Bell notes on Bankrate .com that inflation could aid mortgage holders, but points out that "high inflation has historically hurt the American economy." Bell says that when inflation rises, consumer's purchasing power falls and the standard of living drops. He also says it becomes harder to borrow because lenders raise interest rates to anticipate the cost of inflation.

The viewpoints in the following chapter further examine other benefits and dangers of inflation.

> "Inflation destroys economies, societies,
> and freedoms."

Inflation Destroys Economies

Brad Lyles

*Brad Lyles is a doctor and a writer for the Tea Party. In the follow-
ing viewpoint he argues that governments meddle in the economy
out of ignorance and greed. He says that government interference
in the economy is the cause of inflation. Lyles argues that inflation
is evil, because it hurts people who live on fixed incomes and destroys the economy. He concludes that governments should try to
meddle in the economy as little as possible so that inflation will fall
and freedom will increase.*

As you read, consider the following questions:

1. According to Lyles, why were the theories of economist
   John Maynard Keynes so damaging?
2. What is the Austrian School and what does Lyles say that
   it proposes?
3. How does any government intervention in the economy
   cause inflation, according to Lyles?

"There is no subtler, no surer means of overturning the existing ... society than to debauch the currency (by a continuing process of inflation). (This) process engages all the hidden forces of economic law on the side of destruction, and does it in a manner which not one man in a million is able to diagnose," John Maynard Keynes, 1919 [quoting Russian revolutionary Vladimir Lenin].

Lord Keynes, the celebrated British economist and author of the Keynesian theory of macroeconomics, wrote these prophetic words in 1919, a mere two years after the October Bolshevik Revolution in Russia and only one year following the end of the Great War [World War I]. Astonishingly, this was a time in American history when the U.S. government didn't have the first clue about how to cause inflation.

Keynes, Roosevelt, and State Power

Who cares? You should. Keynes is the father of modern economics. He is also the progenitor of the West's flamboyant proclivity for government intervention into the economy. Keynes was the first of the new breed of scholars of the "dismal science" [that is economics] who promoted government intervention into almost every aspect of a nation's economy, especially in the case of free market economies, as exemplified by the free market economy once present in the United States. It was argued that the State's depredations upon an economy were necessary in order to provide "stability," "security," and (whilst stealing freedom away) "freedom from want."

In the 1930's, at a time when Keynesianism was all the rage, Statist politicians such as [Democratic] President [Franklin] Roosevelt, all three full terms of him, appropriated Keynesian Theory to support every misguided "Program" he could think of on Fridays after watching the young ones play tennis. In fact, it was Roosevelt who fantasized the notorious "Second Bill of Rights," promising a "chicken in every pot"[1] and Freedom from Want and Insecurity all the days of our lives.

And why shouldn't he have so promised? Isn't it true that Keynes' virginal economic theory supported everything Roosevelt was doing? Sadly, yes. Essentially, Keynes, and the preponderance of elite "economics" scholars at the time (and since), signed a blank check for Roosevelt and every succeeding American President, enshrining the populist and popular delusion that somebody else would always pay for the free lunch.

How is it that Keynes was so damaging and how does this relate to you and your pocketbook? Keynes' theory permitted governments to trot out sophisticated theories in support of their indelible aptitude for mucking about with the economy.

For the first time in history, government did not have to exert itself to justify its meddling in the affairs of free individuals and free markets. On the contrary, governments could now prance about with a golden hall pass allowing them as many sleazy financial manipulations as they could imagine—and they have imagined a lot.

Prior to Keynes, the State meddled with national economies but had no academic "expert" justification for doing so. No more! Since Keynes—garrulous government hacks and economics professors have paraded together, lock-step, around the public square, newfound brothers in arms.

Curiously, even when Keynesian Theory was proven wrong in the stagflation of the mid-1960's,[2] both the political and economics gangs joined together to create "modified" Keynesian theory, all brands of which still dictate Statist interventions into a country's economy just so.

Perhaps one explanation for such idiocy from Academe (assuming we'd ever have to explain such a thing) is the fact that for the first time in history, the political elite actually invited the otherwise socially ostracized economics nerds into their councils and their parties, as long as the nerds continued to justify what the political elites were already doing—screwing with the economy.

At all times prior, (other than for [Karl] Marx and Russia), the notion of central control of an economy was cast aside as unrealistic and unsellable. Who in their right mind would vote to allow a bunch of partisan politicians to wield control over a nation's lifeblood—its economy?

Following in the wake of Keynes and his followers, however, American voters voted for just this—to empower government to take comprehensive control of the nation's economy. Geez. They should be able to trust the Professors, shouldn't they?

Keynes Refuted

Nowadays, even though Keynesian theory has been refuted on virtually all grounds, as have its "fellow traveler" theories, government apparatchiks persist in trading upon it to justify their every political whim. And, woe be to the political analyst foolish enough to suggest that government control might not be such a great idea on a priori grounds alone. Such a one is pilloried and marginalized immediately following his first talk-show appearance.

Moreover, in a Society where free speech is flaunted, any questioning of the reigning macroeconomic Statist-in-charge doctrine is met with punishment both swift and severe, if unseen. How could it be otherwise? What else would likely happen to someone who questions BOTH the political elites AND the academic elites of our country at the same time?

Given the Complicit Media's death-grip upon the flow of ideas in the U.S., most people don't know that "Keynesian," "Classical," "Neo-Keynesian," and "Monetarist" economic theories, the ones justifying government mucking about with the economy, are NOT the only economic theories germane to Western democratic economies. These theories are NOT the only rigorously derived theories, i.e. the kind that use confusing mathematics to support their claims.

On the contrary, there exists a body of research and writing entirely foreign to Keynesian postulates. It is known as the "Austrian School" (of economics). It has also been referred to as the supply side or free markets school of economics.

Essentially, the Austrian School proposes that even though common sense is not so common it nevertheless applies to economic systems:

a) Letting any power, especially the State, control ANY aspect of the economy is no better than letting the fox guard the henhouse.

b) Lord Acton was right: "Power corrupts . . ." In other words, even if one were to permit only honorable politicians (oxymoron?) to manipulate the economy, the siren songs of such power would inevitably corrupt them anyway.

c) Freedom Works. In other words, government's role in an economy is best limited to staying out of the way and enforcing legal transactions, and that's it.

Is it any wonder that Austrian economics is NOT the most popular dinner topic at government or academic functions? Compliance with Austrian principles would at once eliminate at least 50% of the Economics Departments in the U.S., eliminate 95% of the government bureaucracy's power, and, worst of all, it would strand almost all of Academe's economists in the foyer, all dressed up and no place to go.

It is notable that Austrian economic theory arrived on the scene in 1922 (Mises' Socialism), fully eleven years before Keynes' magnum opus and only five years after the Russian Revolution of 1917. Admittedly, Marx, and his Communist Manifesto, went public in 1848. Nevertheless, Austrian economics was in large measure based upon the far earlier work of Adam Smith (*Wealth of Nations*, 1776). Smith is commonly referred to as the Father of Capitalism and free markets.

"Hey, wait a second!" you're likely thinking, "didn't the Founders envision free markets for America?" Yes! You get an A! In fact, the Founders intended that our government be permitted the least possible entree into America's economy and markets. The Founders were well-acquainted with governments that did otherwise, say, for example, Great Britain, and did not wish for America to fall prey to the same wealth-destroying structures plaguing most every other country at the time. Hmmm. Where did we go wrong?!

To be clear, the Austrian School of economics advocates for the central tenet of our nation's founding—FREEDOM. It declares that economic liberty is not merely Liberty—it is the surest path to the enrichment of the entire society. On the contrary, it declares that government intervention, whether Communist, Socialist, or any color in between, is the surest path to impoverishment—for all.

Inflation

What about INFLATION? Inflation is the inevitable result of government intervention, any government intervention, into the economy. Why? Because when our government spends money (from taxes, selling Treasury Bills, or by printing dollars), it provides a net loss to the economy. By subtracting value from the economy, or by injecting unearned dollars into the economy, our economy ends up with less "product" and more dollars—hence the price of everything goes up.

Like radioactivity after the nuke, inflation eats up the value of pensions and retirement savings. The 10% "real" inflation rate we have now means that your grandmother's likely going to be dining on cat food next year because the $500.00 per month she spends on groceries now will cost $550.00 next year; everything will cost more next year. If a person lives on a "fixed income," say, like Social Security, (and without the COLA's[3]) inflation is a knife to the heart.

We've come full circle. We know that inflation destroys an economy—and we know how—just as Lenin and Keynes predicted it would. We also know that paradoxically (for the Keynesian), any government intervention into an economy causes inflation, and at best provides a net loss for the economy. We also know that in the 1930's, Keynes unwittingly sponsored the unholy union of politicians and economists that got us where we are today: Perpetually bending over and hoping the spanking won't be so bad this time.

Regardless, politicians, economists, and media cheerleaders are nowadays so brazen in their own self-interest as to mouth the words, "Stimulus," "Jobs Bill," "Bail-Out," "QE II" and "QE III,"[4] as if these words actually meant something. Instead, these shills mislead the electorate and every sophist creature plays along.

Finally, we return to Keynes' prophetic words: "There is no subtler, no surer means of overturning the existing . . . society than . . . inflation." So, why would our political, academic and media elites want to cause inflation and destroy our Society? Take your pick: Greed ("it's always about the money"), avarice, ambition, idealism, malice, "good intentions," whatever. Regardless of the reason, the result is still the same: Destruction of our Society. Because of such phenomena, Lord Acton concluded that, in addition to power corrupting, "absolute power corrupts absolutely."

So, the next time you see someone smirk superciliously about the necessity of Quantitative Easing or of having the Fed lower interest rates below market levels, or a "Stimulus," or even a "Jobs Bill," simply smirk back and ask, "So you agree with Lenin, do you?"

Inflation destroys economies, societies and freedoms. All governments are inflationary. Some government functions are necessary. Accordingly, some inflation is necessary—unavoidable—but not by much.

Notes

1. A slogan used by Republicans in the 1928 Presidential campaign.
2. Stagflation is when both unemployment and inflation are high. The term was coined in the mid-1960s, but generally is used in reference to economic conditions in the 1970s.
3. COLA is cost of living adjustment. It is an automatic increase in fixed incomes every year to keep up with inflation.
4. The stimulus and jobs bill are government spending programs meant to reduce unemployment. QE is quantitative easing, a Federal Reserve program to increase the money supply and stimulate the economy.

"High inflation is harmful, but moderate inflation (up to 40%) is not only not necessarily harmful, but may even be compatible with rapid growth and employment creation."

Preventing Inflation Can Stifle an Economy

Ha-Joon Chang

Ha-Joon Chang is a reader in the political economy of development at the University of Cambridge. In the following viewpoint, he argues that low interest rates, which promote moderate inflation, make the cost of investment relatively cheap, and thus encourage growth and prosperity. He argues that the financial industry benefits from price stability, and suggests that this is why central bankers and policymakers often argue for low inflation. However, he says, developing countries should embrace moderate inflation to improve living standards.

As you read, consider the following questions:

1. According to Chang, what statistics from Brazil indicate that inflation does not hurt growth?

2. What does Chang say is the only way for South Africa to reduce the huge gap in living standards between racial groups?

3. Why does Chang say that it is a myth that central bankers are nonpartisan technocrats?

Inflation is bad for growth—this has become one of the most widely accepted economic nostrums of our age. But see how you feel about it after digesting the following piece of information.

Inflation in Brazil and Korea

During the 1960s and the 1970s, Brazil's average inflation rate was 42% a year. Despite this, Brazil was one of the fastest growing economies in the world for those two decades—its *per capita* income grew at 4.5% a year during this period. In contrast, between 1996 and 2005, during which time Brazil embraced the neo-liberal orthodoxy,[1] especially in relation to macroeconomic policy, its inflation rate averaged a much lower 7.1% a year. But during this period, *per capita* in Brazil grew at only 1.3% a year.

If you are not entirely persuaded by the Brazilian case—understandable, given that hyperinflation went side by side with low growth in the 1980s and the early 1990s—how about this? During its 'miracle' years, when its economy was growing at 7% a year in *per capita* terms, Korea had inflation rates close to 20%–17.4% in the 1960s and 19.8% in the 1970s. These were rates higher than those found in several Latin American countries, and totally contrary to the cultural stereotypes of the hyper-saving, prudent East Asian versus fun-loving, profligate Latinos. . . . In the 1960s Korea's inflation rate was *much higher* than that of five Latin America countries (Venezuela, Bolivia, Mexico, Peru and Colombia) and not much lower than that infamous 'rebel teenager', Argentina. In the 1970s, the Korean inflation rate was higher than that found in Venezuela, Ecuador and Mexico, and not much lower than that of Colombia and

Bolivia. Are you still convinced that inflation is incompatible with economic success?

With these examples, I am not arguing that all inflation is good. When prices rise very fast, they undermine the very basis of rational economic calculation. The experience of Argentina in the 1980s and the early 1990s is quite illustrative in this regard. In January 1977, a carton of milk cost 1 peso. Fourteen years later, the same container cost over 1 billion pesos. Between 1977 and 1991, inflation ran at an annual rate of 333%. There was a twelve-month period, ending in 1990, during which actual inflation was 20,266%. The story has it that, during this period, prices rose so fast that some supermarkets resorted to using blackboards rather than price tags. There is no question that this kind of price inflation makes long-range planning impossible. Without a reasonably long time-horizon, rational investment decisions become impossible. And without robust investment, economic growth becomes very difficult.

Hyperinflation vs. Inflation

But there is a big logical jump between acknowledging the destructive nature of hyperinflation and arguing that the lower the rate of inflation, the better. As the examples of Brazil and Korea show, the inflation rate does not have to be in the 1–3% range, as Stanley Fischer [governor of the Bank of Israel] and most neo-liberals want, for an economy to do well. Indeed, even many neo-liberal economists admit that, below 10%, inflation does not seem to have any adverse effect on economic growth. Two World Bank economists, Michael Bruno, once the chief economist, and William Easterly, have shown that, below 40%, there is no systematic correlation between a country's inflation rate and its growth rate. They even argue that, below 20%, higher inflation seemed to be associated with higher growth during some time periods.

In other words, there is inflation and there is inflation. High inflation is harmful, but moderate inflation (up to 40%) is not only not necessarily harmful, but may even be compatible with rapid growth and employment creation. We may even say that some degree of inflation is inevitable in a dynamic economy. Prices change because the economy changes, so it is natural that prices go up in an economy where there are lots of new activities creating new demand.

But, if moderate inflation is not harmful, why are neo-liberals so obsessed with it? Neo-liberals would argue that all inflation—moderate or not—is still objectionable, because it disproportion-ately hurts people on fixed incomes—notably wage earners and pensioners, who are the most vulnerable sections of the popula-tion. Paul Volcker, the chairman of the US Federal Reserve Board (the US central bank) under Ronald Reagan (1979–87), argued: 'Inflation is thought of as a cruel, and maybe the cruellest, tax because it hits in a many-sectored way, in an unplanned way, and it hits the people on a fixed income hardest'.

But this is only half the story. Lower inflation may mean that what the workers have already earned is better protected, but the policies that are needed to generate this outcome may reduce what they can earn in the future. Why is this? The tight monetary and fiscal policies that are needed to lower inflation, especially to a very low level, are likely also to reduce the level of economic activity, which, in turn, will lower the demand for labour and thus increase unemployment and reduce wages. So a tough con-trol on inflation is a two-edged sword for workers—it protects their existing incomes better, but it reduces their future incomes. It is only the pensioners and others (including, significantly, the financial industry) whose incomes derive from financial assets with fixed returns for whom lower inflation is a pure blessing. Since they are outside the labour market, tough macroeconomic policies that lower inflation cannot adversely affect their future employment opportunities and wages, while the incomes they already have are better protected.

Neo-liberals have made a big deal out of the fact that infla-tion hurts the general public, as we can see from the earlier quote

Low Inflation Increases Banking Crises

One sense in which the world has become more unstable during the last three decades of free-market dominance and strong anti-inflationary policies is the increased frequency and extent of financial crises. According to a study by Kenneth Rogoff, a former chief economist of the IMF and now a professor at Harvard University, and Carmen Reinhart, a professor at the University of Maryland, virtually no country was in banking crisis between the end of the Second World War and the mid 1970s, when the world was much more unstable than today, when measured by inflation. Between the mid 1970s and the late 1980s, when inflation accelerated in many countries, the proportion of countries with banking crises rose to 5–10 per cent, weighted by their share of world income, seemingly confirming the inflation-centric view of the world. However, the proportion of countries with banking crises shot up to around 20 per cent in the mid 1990s, when we are supposed to have finally tamed the beast called inflation and attained the elusive goal of economic stability. The ratio then briefly fell to zero for a few years in the mid 2000s, but went up again to 35 per cent following the 2008 global financial crisis (and is likely to rise even further at the time of writing, that is, early 2010).

Ha-Joon Chang, 23 Things They Don't Tell You about Capitalism. *New York: Bloomsbury Press, 2010.*

from Volcker. But this populist rhetoric obscures the fact that the policies needed to generate low inflation are likely to reduce the future earnings of most working people by reducing their employment prospects and wage rates.

The Cost of Price Stability

Upon taking power from the apartheid regime in 1994, the new ANC (African National Congress) government of South Africa declared that it would pursue an IMF [International Monetary Fund]-style macroeconomic policy.[2] Such a cautious approach was considered necessary if it was not to scare away investors, given its leftwing, revolutionary history.

In order to maintain price stability, interest rates [the price of borrowing money] were kept high; at their peak in the late 1990s and the early 2000s, the real interest rates were 10–12%. Thanks to such tight monetary policy, the country has been able to keep its inflation rate during this period at 6.3% a year. But this was achieved at a huge cost to growth and jobs. Given that the average non-financial firm in South Africa has a profit rate of less than 6%, real interest rates of 10–12% meant that few firms could borrow to invest. No wonder the investment rate (as a proportion of GDP) fell from the historical 20–25% (it was once over 30% in the early 1980s) down to about 15%. Considering such low levels of investment, the South African economy has not done too badly—between 1994 and 2005, its *per capita* income grew at 1.8% a year. But that is only 'considering . . .'

Unless South Africa is going to engage in a major programme of redistribution (which is neither politically feasible nor economically wise), the only way to reduce the huge gap in living standards between the racial groups in the country is to generate rapid growth and create more jobs, so that more people can join the economic mainstream and improve their living standards. Currently [2008], the country has an *official* unemployment rate of 26–8%, one of the highest in the world; a 1.8% annual growth rate is way too inadequate to bring about a serious reduction in unemployment and poverty. In the last few years, the South African government has thankfully seen the folly of this approach and has brought the interest rates down, but real interest rates, at around 8%, are still too high for vigorous investment.

In most countries, firms outside the financial sector make a 3–7% profit. Therefore, if real interest is above that level, it makes more sense for potential investors to put their money in the bank, or buy bonds, rather than invest it in a productive firm. Also taking into account all the trouble involved in managing productive enterprises—labour problems, problems with delivery of parts, trouble with payments by customers, etc.—the threshold rate may even be lower. Given that firms in developing countries have little capital accumulated internally, making borrowing more difficult means that firms cannot invest much. This results in low investment, which, in turn, means low growth and scarce jobs. This is what has happened in Brazil, South Africa and numerous other developing countries when they followed the Bad Samaritans' [rich Western countries] advice and pursued a very low rate of inflation.

Rich Countries and Interest Rates

However, the reader would be surprised to learn that the rich Bad Samaritan countries, which are so keen to preach to developing countries the importance of high real interest rates as a key to monetary discipline, themselves have resorted to lax monetary policies when they have needed to generate income and jobs. At the height of their post-Second-World-War growth boom, real interest rates in the rich countries were all very low—or even negative. Between 1960 and '73, the latter half of the 'Golden Age of Capitalism' (1950–73), when all of today's rich nations achieved high investment and rapid growth, the average real interest rates were 2.6% in Germany, 1.8% in France, 1.5% in the USA, 1.4% in Sweden and −1.0% in Switzerland.

Monetary policy[3] that is too tight [where interest rates are high] lowers investment. Lower investment slows down growth and job creation. This may not be a huge problem for rich countries with already high standards of living, generous welfare state provision and low poverty, but it is a disaster for developing countries that desperately need more income and jobs and often are trying to deal with a high degree of income inequality without resorting to a large-scale redistribution programme that, anyway, may create more problems than it solves.

Central Banks Must Be Accountable

Given the costs of pursuing a restrictive monetary policy, giving independence to the central bank with the sole aim of controlling inflation is the last thing a developing country should do, because it will institutionally entrench monetarist macroeconomic policy that is particularly unsuitable for developing countries. This is all the more so when there is actually *no* clear evidence that greater central bank independence even lowers the rate of inflation in developing countries, let alone helps to achieve other desirable aims, like higher growth and lower unemployment.

It is a myth that central bankers are non-partisan technocrats. It is well known that they tend to listen very closely to the view of the financial sector and implement policies that help it, if necessary at the cost of the manufacturing industry or wage-earners. So, giving them independence allows them to pursue policies that benefit their own natural constituencies without appearing to do so. The policy bias would be even worse if we explicitly tell them that they should not worry about any policy objectives other than inflation.

Moreover, central bank independence raises an important issue for democratic accountability. The flip side of the argument that central bankers can take good decisions only because their jobs do not depend on making the electorate happy is that they can pursue policies that hurt the majority of people with impunity—especially if they are told not to worry about anything other than the rate of inflation. Central bankers need to be supervised by elected politicians, so that they can be, even if at one remove, responsive to the popular will. This is exactly why the charter of the US Federal Reserve Board defines its first responsibility as 'conducting the nation's monetary policy by influencing the monetary and credit conditions in the economy in pursuit of *maximum employment, stable prices, and moderate long-term interest rates* [italics added]' and why the Fed chairman is subject to regular grilling by Congress. Ironic, then, that the US government acts internationally as a Bad Samaritan and encourages developing countries to create an independent central bank solely focused on inflation.

Notes

1. Neoliberalism is an economic philosophy that argues for the efficiency of private enterprise and low inflation.
2. Macroeconomic Policy is economic policy relating to the whole economy. The IMF is an organization of 187 countries, that promotes economic cooperation. It usually pushes for low inflation.
3. Monetary policy is the control of the money supply, usually by raising or lowering interest rules.

> "It's important to remember that
> the global economy is still largely
> dependent on China."

Inflation in China Will
Exacerbate the Global
Recession

Shah Gilani

Shah Gilani is a market analyst and the writer of the Capital Wave
Forecast *newsletter. In the following viewpoint he argues that inflation in China has reached dangerous levels. He says that the
Chinese government needs to control inflation, but that its efforts
to do so may result in a dangerous slowing of the Chinese economy.
Gilani says that this is especially dangerous because China's growth
has been the main engine driving the world economy for the past
several years. Gilani says that a setback in the Chinese economy
could cause a painful worldwide financial slowdown.*

As you read, consider the following questions:

1. What worrisome statistics does Gilani present about food
   price inflation in China?

2. According to Gilani, what has China done in relation to banks in order to control inflation?

3. What policy does Gilani say would have the effect of a sledgehammer on China's export industry?

Inflation in China is far more intractable than official headline statistics reveal.

China's Biggest Problem

That's potentially bad news for global growth and toppy [that is, reaching their top] stock and commodities markets.

If China effectively dampens dangerously high inflationary expectations and real, rapidly rising food, property and fixed-investment assets by hitting the brakes too hard, global growth could skid and potentially stall out.

The resulting sound of breaking glass would likely be clear support levels enjoyed by rising stock and commodity markets as they finally correct [that is, fall], along with theories of China's infinite growth trajectory.

Even China's Statistics Bureau has said consumer inflation growth is "too fast." And, Vice Premier Wang Qishun recently called inflation "China's biggest problem."

April's [2011] headline consumer price index (CPI) reading just came in at 5.3%, well above the official target rate of 4%. The CPI compares current price levels with year-ago levels.

Even though April's CPI number came in above Wall Street's consensus estimate of 5.2% and higher than Beijing's official projection, a sigh of relief was breathed that the rate was lower than March's 5.4% level, which itself was a two-year high.

Still, looking at inflation statistics through a short historical prism indicates much deeper problems.

In 2008, rapid growth in China and rising commodity and food prices around the globe pushed consumer inflation in China to 5.5%. The rate subsequently fell to an approximate rate of -1% at the depth of the credit crisis in March 2009. However, it has since risen steadily, and is once again nearing 5.5%.

Food price inflation (FPI) is far more chilling. Chinese food inflation reached 22.5% back in 2008. And like the overall trend of inflation in China, FPI has been on a steep trajectory higher since bottoming out in 2009. In fact, it just reached a worrisome 11.5% in April, making for the sixth straight month of double-digit gains.

Non-food CPI was up 2.7% in April, the same as in March, and the highest it's been in five years.

More Bad News

And there's even more bad news.

For the January–April period of this year, fixed-asset investment growth was 25.4% higher than the same period a year ago. Additionally, residential investment rose a staggering 38.6% over the same four-month period, according to Moody's Analytics.

The problem facing China is how to foster growth robust enough to keep its huge and growing workforce employed without stoking dangerous levels of inflation. A failure to succeed in either respect could trigger civil unrest.

It's important to remember that the global economy is still largely dependent on China.

China for the past few years has been a powerful engine of economic growth that's helped both emerging markets and developed nations rebound from the global financial crisis. If its economy stalls, the impact will be global.

Indeed, Chinese growth is what's truly been driving the world's equity and commodity markets, as well as many bond markets.

With stimulus packages being reined in around the globe, the U.S. Federal Reserve slowly backing off from quantitative easing, and central banks around the world raising interest rates,[1] China's continuing growth is the only fuel still feeding hope and speculation.

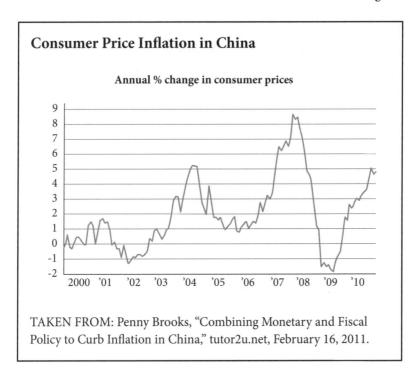

Consumer Price Inflation in China

Annual % change in consumer prices

TAKEN FROM: Penny Brooks, "Combining Monetary and Fiscal Policy to Curb Inflation in China," tutor2u.net, February 16, 2011.

If China makes one wrong move, the interconnectedness of economies and overly correlated market plays could quickly test the one-world economy.

The Chinese government's approach so far has been—and should continue to be—targeted and broad-range attacks on the inflationary menace. And so far they've been measured.

On the "targeted" front, reserve requirements [the amount of money banks must hold] have been raised. The theory is that by forcing banks to hold more reserves, less money will make its way through the system to feed rising prices.

Additionally, the key interest rate has been hiked four times since October [2010]. By jacking China's one-year benchmark interest rate up to 6.31%, the central bank is essentially throwing a wet blanket over the entire economy. Higher interest rates are more of a blunt instrument than a targeted smart-bomb.

Still, inflation seems to be entrenched.

A Sledgehammer to Exports

There is another weapon the government has, but it would have the effect of a sledgehammer on China's vibrant export industry. That would be allowing China's currency, the yuan, to appreciate [rise in price] more than the piddling 5% rise it's had against the dollar over the past year. That would certainly dampen inflation—both in real terms and expectations.

However, the cost of such a move would be difficult to absorb. So that hoped for approach isn't really in the playbook, and won't be for a year or three.

We're already seeing fallout from a mere perceived slowing in China. Oil has dipped on expectations that China might raise rates again. China's imports of iron ore were down 11% in April from March, and were 4% lower year-over-year. Copper imports were down 14% from March to April and down a whopping 40% year-over-year. So is it any wonder that iron ore and copper prices have fallen?

Trillions of dollars have flowed not just into China, but into the raw materials and commodities that have fueled the country's growth and the stocks of corporations that have benefited from its increased consumption.

Now, its capital flows will have to be closely watched.

The minute large capital flows start to move, as they do rapidly in the new world economy, investors need to be watching where money is coming out and where it's being repositioned.

Right now, all eyes should be on China's inflation-fighting policies and actions. With markets bumping up against recent highs and leveraged speculation rampant, any attack on inflation that takes too much air out of China's pumped-up growth rates could flush out weak hands in a matter of weeks, if not days.

Note

1. Stimulus packages are government spending programs. Central banks try to stimulate the economy through lowering interest rates.

"China's average inflation rate of
2% over the past ten years has been
unusually low for a developing
country."

Inflation in China Will Help
Both China and the World

Economist

The Economist *is a weekly British news and business magazine.
The following viewpoint argues that growing inflation in China
may actually help to balance the Chinese economy. The Economist argues that China has too little consumption. The magazine
says that inflation would encourage workers to save less and spend
more. Inflation would also, says the* Economist, *help to effectively
lower the value of the yuan and reduce China's trade surplus. The*
Economist *also argues that the threat of runaway inflation in
China is small, so moderate inflation should be welcomed.*

As you read, consider the following questions:

1. What is the Balassa-Samuelson effect, according to the
   Economist?
2. How much has the yuan risen against the dollar since
   2009 by the *Economist's* calculations?

3. To what countries does the *Economist* compare China, and why do these comparisons suggest that runaway inflation is not a serious threat?

China's inflation rate has become one of the world's most closely watched numbers. This week's release showed that inflation rose to 4.9% in January [2011], up from 1.5% a year earlier. The increase was smaller than expected, but has not quelled fears that as inflation creeps up the government will need to slam on the economic brakes. Some economists, however, believe that China should welcome higher inflation as a more effective way to rebalance its economy than a currency appreciation [a rise in the purchasing power of China's money].

Rebalancing China

The recent surge in Chinese inflation has been driven mainly by food prices, but non-food inflation has also risen to 2.6%, its highest rate since the series began in 2001. Wages are increasing at a faster rate. For many years China's large pool of surplus labour held average pay rises below the rate of productivity growth. But as fewer young people enter the workforce, wages are now rising faster than productivity. Arthur Kroeber of Dragonomics, a Beijing-based research firm, argues that if higher inflation reflects faster wage growth, this will help China, not hurt it.

Economists brought up to believe inflation is always a bad thing will choke on the idea of welcoming more of it, but the truth is that China's average inflation rate of 2% over the past ten years has been unusually low for a developing country [see chart]. The optimal inflation rate in an emerging economy is often higher than in the developed world because of something called the "Balassa-Samuelson effect". As low-income countries catch up with richer ones, faster productivity growth in the tradable-goods sector pushes up wages. Since labour is mobile, this in turn leads to higher wages in the non-tradable sector, where productivity growth is slower, so prices rise faster than

in rich countries. Moreover, some of the ways in which inflation is thought to be harmful to growth, such as discouraging
saving and investment, hardly matter in China, where both look
excessive.

Indeed, a bit more inflation could help to rebalance China's
lopsided economy. Its biggest imbalance is too little consumption, largely because wages have fallen as a share of national
income. When wages rise more slowly than productivity, an
economy produces more than it can consume, resulting in a
current-account surplus.[1] If wages now outpace productivity,
workers' share of the cake will rise, boosting consumption and
helping to reduce China's external surplus.

Trade Surplus

Wage-driven inflation would also help to narrow China's trade
surplus by pushing up the price of its exports. Conventional
wisdom says that a stronger yuan would reduce China's current-
account surplus.[2] Yet the empirical support for this is weak. In
a paper published in 2009, Menzie Chinn of the University of
Wisconsin and Shang-Jin Wei of Columbia University examined
more than 170 countries over the period 1971–2005, and found
little evidence that countries with flexible exchange rates reduced
their current-account imbalances more quickly than countries
with more rigid regimes.

In adjusting current accounts, what matters is the real exchange rate (which takes account of relative inflation rates at
home and abroad). Movements in nominal exchange rates often do not achieve the desired adjustment in real rates because
they may be offset by changing domestic prices. For example, the
yen's trade-weighted value is around 150% stronger than it was
in 1985. Yet Japan's current-account surplus remains big because
that appreciation has been largely offset by a fall in domestic
Japanese wholesale prices, so exporters remain competitive.

An alternative way to lift a real exchange rate is through higher
inflation than abroad. To an American buyer, a 5% increase in the

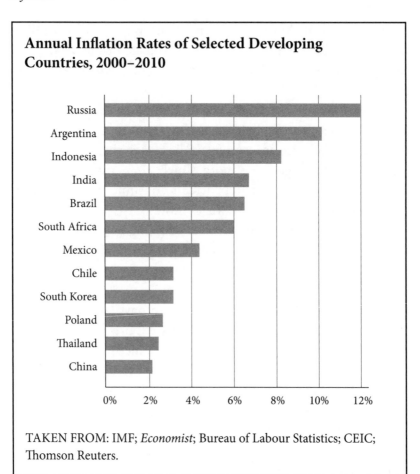

Annual Inflation Rates of Selected Developing Countries, 2000–2010

TAKEN FROM: IMF; *Economist*; Bureau of Labour Statistics; CEIC; Thomson Reuters.

yuan price of Chinese exports is the same as a 5% appreciation of the yuan against the dollar. Mr. Kroeber argues that rebalancing the economy by running an inflation rate of 4–6% would be preferable to either a sharp increase in the yuan, which could cause big job losses in export firms, or a gradual appreciation which attracted large speculative capital inflows, as happened in 2005–08. Inflation is already playing the bigger role. The yuan has risen by only 4% against the dollar since early 2009, yet, according to calculations by the *Economist*, the yuan's real exchange rate against the dollar (measured using unit labour costs in industry) has strengthened by 17%, because costs in China are rising much faster than in America.

The Runaway Risk

What about the risk that inflation could get out of control, as in Latin America in the 1980s and 1990s or in China itself in 1989, when an inflation rate of over 25% triggered unrest? Runaway inflation is usually the result of fiscal excess, financed by printing money, or rigid labour markets, which produce a wage-price spiral that the central bank fails to stop. Unlike Latin America in the past, China has a record of fiscal prudence and trade unions are docile. Its labour market is much more flexible than in the late 1980s, when most workers were in the state sector.

China is more like Japan and South Korea during their eras of rapid growth than any Latin American country. Over 15-year periods ending in Japan in 1972 and South Korea in 1996, GDP [gross domestic product] growth averaged around 9% a year and inflation averaged 5–6% without it accelerating out of control. China's government cannot be complacent about rising prices. It should anchor expectations by setting an explicit inflation target. Interest rates on bank deposits need to be raised in line with inflation to encourage households to keep their money in the bank rather than speculate in property or shares. Otherwise negative real interest rates will inflate asset bubbles. That implies China still needs a more flexible exchange rate so it can lift interest rates while those in America remain low. But a bit more inflation would be welcome as well.

Notes

1. The current account is a measure of foreign trade. A current account surplus means a country is increasing its share of foreign assets.
2. If China's currency were stronger, paying workers in China would be relatively more expensive. Goods from China would then be more expensive to make, and so people would buy fewer goods from China, balancing trade.

> "In light of current and prospective upward pressure on the relative price of food, policy officials should move away from measures that control and hence distort prices experienced by consumers and producers."

Inflation in Worldwide Food Prices Hurts the Poor

Karen H. Johnson

Karen H. Johnson is a consulting economist at the Council on Foreign Relations. In the following viewpoint she says that food prices have been rising alarmingly over the past few years. She says that this increase seems to be caused by increased demand for food in the developing world. She says that if not addressed, increased prices may cause hardship and hunger. She recommends a lowering of trade barriers, an end to agricultural subsidies, and a move away from policies that distort the market. She argues that such policies will help encourage food production and therefore help control food prices in the long term.

As you read, consider the following questions:

1. According to Johnson, in the 2008 crop year, how far above the previous five-year average were prices for wheat, corn, and rice?
2. Why does Johnson say that price controls are a poor monetary policy for controlling inflation of food prices?
3. What are the three pillars of the Doha strategy, according to Johnson?

Increases in the prices for major food crops that are traded globally have reached extraordinary levels, sparking riots in some countries and becoming the focus of widespread debate and policy concern. During the current crop year, [2008] the price for wheat is nearly 90 percent above its average for the preceding five years, that for corn 60 percent, and that for rice more than 35 percent. At the June summit meeting of the UN's Food and Agricultural Organization in Rome, officials from around the world engaged in discussions of who or what is to blame.

The sharp moves up in food prices have contributed to the acceleration in overall consumer prices and are cited by many officials, along with energy prices, as factors in pushing inflation rates above desired levels. Higher inflation has become a concern among central banks in the industrial and the emerging market economies, and possible tightening of monetary policy [raising interest rates to decrease the money supply] is again being discussed. . . .

Demand Outstripping Supply

The balance of demand and supply since 2003 for the major food crops (wheat, corn, rice, and soybeans) has been such that inventories held around the world of these foods has, on balance, moved down. These stocks are now significantly lower than they were from 1990 to 2002, an interval during which they fluctuated narrowly. In 2003 and again in 2004, aggregate stocks stepped down to reach a lower level around which they have since fluctuated.

The overall picture of demand and supply since 2003 is thus one in which supply has grown but not matched demand. As a consequence, some of the demand has been met by a drawdown of stocks held in inventory. Nevertheless, prices have been bid up by demand as markets have needed higher prices to match demand to the available supply plus change in inventory. As inventory stocks decrease, so does the available buffer they provide to unexpected strength in demand. As a result, prices have a tendency to move sharply in response to demand surprises. With prices high and rising, all those in the market have an incentive to hold inventories in order to sell later at a higher price (suppliers) or to avoid having to pay more in the future (demanders). Despite these incentives, recorded inventories have moved down, supporting the view that demand has generally been stronger than supply over this period. Of course, some inventories may be held by households or even distributors in ways that escape measurement. Stories this year about rice, for example, suggest that users who feared short supplies purchased large amounts and actually accelerated the appearance of inadequate supply and bid up the price. Over time, as these unseen inventories reach the levels needed to reassure consumers, demand and price both drop. We have seen some of that occurring in the most recent price developments.

Review of the demand and supply factors behind the upward trend in prices since 2003 suggests that rising demand has been the major determinant behind the higher prices, though some supply factors, including diversion of resources for ethanol production,[1] have contributed as well. For many crops, supply has been steady, not falling, as it would need to be if supply-side problems were the primary reason for the rise in prices. The most important demand element—the shift in global growth on the margin to developing and emerging market economies—is likely to persist for some time. The adjustment forces that will

World Food Consumption (million metric tons)

World food consumption is rising. This is helping to push up food prices.

	2003–04	2004–05	2005–06	2006–07	2007–08
Wheat	589	607	625	616	622
Corn	649	689	706	728	779
Rice	414	409	416	420	426

TAKEN FROM: Karen H. Johnson, "Food Price Inflation: Explanation and Policy Implications," Council on Foreign Relations, July 2008, p. 8.

ultimately slow potential growth in these regions and lower their higher consumption of food are not likely to appear for many years. Until then, economic development in these countries will give rise to incremental global food demand. Of the supply factors, some, such as drought, may prove transitory. Others, such as managing the global need for more energy, particularly renewable energy, which competes for many of the same resources that produce food, and raising yields in the developing and emerging regions toward the levels achieved in more advanced regions, are difficult to foresee with any precision. However, in many respects, these elements of the problem are open to policy measures that could have important effects on how food prices behave in the future.

Policy Implications

It seems very unlikely that over the next five to ten years global food prices will retrace the increases that occurred since 2003 and return to the level of prices at that time. A resumption of a trend of slow decline in the relative price of traded food also seems unlikely, though it cannot be ruled out. Futures markets generally call for the prices of traded food commodities to stop rising, but to remain elevated near their current levels. However, the review of demand and supply forces above identifies persistent demand and supply elements that should work to raise prices. The most effective element in raising supply and lowering price, an increase in yields in producing countries, is likely to be slow moving. Accordingly, a scenario with global food prices remaining quite volatile but ratcheting up in episodes over time, resulting in an upward trend over the next decade, appears to have sufficient probability that policy officials should incorporate such an outcome into their planning. Just how volatile food prices prove to be, and how strong the upward trend might be, depend in part on how the related problems of climate change, water availability, and energy resources are managed. The challenge for policy is not a statistical one of analyzing past and current data and looking for evidence of a change. It is rather a judgment call, in which analysis of the reasons for recent events are examined in an effort to draw forward-looking implications.

Monetary Policy

With respect to monetary policy, a switch from a persistent, if only slight, downward trend in the global relative price of food to an upward trend (or even to an unchanged relative price) calls for a change in central bank tactics. The overall policy objective of price stability remains for central banks as does the fundamental central bank responsibility for whatever inflation outcome occurs over the medium term. If the relative price of food continues to move upward over an extended period, it will impart upward pressure on inflation; this is not a one-time shock that moves the price level but drops quickly out of measured inflation. If central banks are to achieve goals of moderate or low inflation over the medium term, they will need to adjust their tactics to allow for rising food prices.

One tempting but counterproductive tactic for controlling inflation of food prices is price control [having the government set the price of food by law]. Often the intent of the controls is not to be an inflation-fighting tool but a social policy. In some countries, governments use price controls on particular food items, usually local staples, as a subsidy to lower-income households (similar policies are also used for fuel). In other countries, price controls have been put on in an effort to moderate a sudden sharp jump in prices. In the event that the relative price of food does continue to rise for a time, such policies can prove very expensive for the government budget and usually will have to be abandoned. At that point, the jump in the price of the previously protected item is large. The result is a sharp rise in the measured inflation rate and political outcry over the shock to household budgets. As a tactic for addressing the inflationary consequences of a change in the trend of global food prices, such controls are ill advised.

For most central banks, the challenge is to incorporate the outlook for global food prices into the forecast for the domestic economy and the overall inflation rate. Food prices pose particular risks to price stability because of their visibility and importance to households. Inflation expectations are central to stabilizing the trend in overall consumer prices and, should they become unanchored, can be very difficult to bring back down. Households do business in food markets more frequently than in any other sector and update their information about what is happening to food prices continuously. If the relative price of food does rise for an extended period, households will need to see convincing evidence that it is only a relative change, and that other prices are declining, if they are to maintain stable inflation expectations. Otherwise, the perception of a step-up in inflation is likely to lead to upward pressure on nominal wages. Once a wage-price spiral sets in, the cost to the economy for the central bank to regain control over prices is higher still.

The possibility that the trend behavior of food prices has changed for a time suggests that the practice of the Fed to focus in a tactical sense not on headline inflation but on core inflation (headline inflation excluding food and energy) should be reexamined. The usefulness of core inflation is pragmatic.

With food and energy prices volatile, the past saw more "noise" in headline inflation than in core inflation. But the two series shared an underlying basic trend, so judgment about future inflation was better informed by readings on core inflation. If a turning point in global food prices has been reached over the past five years, and if those prices are now going to rise for some time, omitting them from the measure used to adjust policy in the short run could result in an inflationary bias. The problems posed by short-term volatility in food and energy prices will likely remain, and some method must be devised to filter out the noise in headline inflation, but it is no longer wise to disregard this measure. The risk that core inflation may be misleading has risen, and omitting food prices may be precisely the wrong thing to do over the next several years. . . .

Agricultural Policy

Evidence from the past five years shows that we have moved from food surpluses in many regions of the world, surpluses which then became a major element of humanitarian food aid for regions with food shortages, to growing demand for food crops that is outstripping supply and increasing relative prices for food. Most recently, an acute crisis of food availability has emerged that spotlights the issue of food distribution and the impact of the rising prices on the world's poorest people. Over the medium term, however, the focus of policy needs also to include incentives for increases in total supply. It is important that measures taken to address concerns about the distribution of food in the short run do not weaken the market signals to producers to expand supply going forward.

Price controls, discussed earlier in the context of monetary policy, have the negative consequence of lessening the return to producers from expanding supply, hence blunting the incentive the current rise in market prices is creating. In addition, price controls on particular foods are essentially arbitrary. They inevitably will distort the signals on the margin for both consumers and producers to substitute among different foods and between food and nonfood consumption or production. Given the complex linkages across the globe in food production, it is essential that the ability of markets to recognize and act on the best possible trade-offs on both the consumption and production side of the food sector be allowed to work as fully as possible. The linkages of food production to energy supply are particularly complex, with varying rates of substitution possible among crops for use as human food, among some crops as the potential inputs into biofuels, and across different crops as best uses for differing qualities of land. We need to allow the price mechanism to guide these allocations to the greatest extent possible. Both price controls and subsidies distort the information and the incentives consumers and producers face. . . .

With demand for food likely to continue to rise more rapidly, and with stocks low, policies with the potential to enhance supply over time are needed. Research with respect to increasing crop yields is important. With yields varying widely across countries, global production could improve significantly if current information is shared and best techniques are applied. Availability of water is a critical factor in maintaining and raising agricultural production. Detailed discussion of water policy issues is beyond the scope of this report. It should be recognized, however, that the price of water is important in agricultural allocation decisions. Distortion of the price charged to farmers for water is another source of inefficiency that should be avoided. At the same time, policies to improve the quality and security of water resources are likely to be more and more important going forward.

In many countries, poor infrastructure is a factor in limiting agricultural output. Transportation facilities for getting inputs of seed and fertilizer to farmers can be a bottleneck. Similarly, farmers struggle to harvest the crop and transport it to a market. Poor storage facilities for crops result in damage due to rodents or rot. Policies to improve such infrastructure could yield substantial gains in supply over time.

Finally, policies on land use need to be reconsidered in light of the changing balance of supply and demand for food. In some countries, development is reducing the amount of land under cultivation as industrialization spreads and cities grow. In the United States, policies adopted in the past offered farmers payment in return for keeping some fields fallow. Currently, 34.6 million acres are enrolled in this program. Recently, the Agricultural Department announced that it would allow 24 million acres of this land to be opened up for haying and grazing of livestock without penalty to the land owner. This move is intended to help lower the cost of feed for raising livestock and is a move in the right direction. Reconsideration of the entire program and the reasons for withholding land from production is warranted.

Trade Policy

As prices have risen sharply in recent months, some countries have responded with changes to their trade policy for agricultural products, intending to protect households from rising prices, counter inflation, and provide security of food supplies for the population. In some cases, such as India and Indonesia, import tariffs were lowered or removed. Such steps are a move in the direction of allowing the price mechanism and global markets to function with fewer distortions and as such are welcome. In many other cases, however, the moves have been to raise barriers to exports of food crops. Many rice producers in Asia (China, India, Vietnam, and others) have limited or banned exports of rice. Other countries restricting food exports range from Argentina (wheat) to Russia (wheat and barley). Such actions introduce new distortions, result in gaps between domestic prices and global prices that impair incentives and likely encourage hoarding, and raise at least temporarily the global prices for some traded foods higher than they would have otherwise been. In some cases, these measures were put in place only for specific intervals and have begun to expire. For example, restrictions by Cambodia and Vietnam either have been or soon will be lifted.

Although temporary barriers of this kind may not cause lasting damage and may in fact address a short-term crisis, they do so at the expense of importing countries that depend on world markets for food. Moreover, they deprive food producers of access to the world's markets and the gain in relative prices that their output would receive on those markets. They also undercut the confidence of all consumers in the world trade system and its capacity to offer products to all purchasers at nondiscriminatory prices.

Agricultural policy has been a major component of the Doha Round of world trade talks.* Progress has been limited, and success of the round is far from certain. Among the contested issues are reductions in agricultural protection by the major industrial countries, along with reduction of manufacturing and services barriers in emerging market and developing countries. The three pillars of the Doha strategy for agricultural reform are market access, export subsidies and competition, and domestic support. The current change in the outlook for the price of traded food crops relative to that of manufacturers is an opportunity for substantial progress in removing distortions in the global agricultural sector that have been entrenched for decades. The switch from a surplus condition for the major traded grains and some other foods to one of rising global price and demand pressures should allow removal of barriers that limit trade, reduction or elimination of subsidies or price supports within the United States, Europe, and elsewhere, and improved global efficiency in production of food at a much lower political cost than was possible previously. Indeed, with high food prices a growing political issue almost everywhere, the continuation of policies that deliberately raise prices to consumers so as to transfer income to well-off farmers is unconscionable. One hopes that it will soon become politically unsustainable.

---

*The Doha Round, under the WHO, brings together trade negotiators from around the world in a series of negotiations with the goal of achieving a set of mutually agreed measures to improve the flow of world trade.

With energy prices also high and rising, the medium-term outlook for global agricultural trade is not entirely clear. As transportation costs rise, the efficiency of producing and consuming food within local areas increases as well. This may result in a reduction of global trade for some foods. With the prospect of rising relative prices for food crops over the medium term, the importance of allowing global trade to permit the most efficient production of food and the least-cost distribution of food to consumers would seem to be extraordinarily high. Such a liberalization of global agricultural trade likely will also boost incomes in some of the world's poorest countries. Trade negotiators need to redouble their efforts to ensure a successful outcome of the Doha Round and liberalization of agricultural trade.

Officials Should Curb Prices

Review of the evidence and the ongoing debate concerning the rise in global food prices has confirmed several points:

- The nominal price of globally traded food . . . has accelerated starting in 2003 and has since been rising at double-digit annual rates. The price of globally traded food relative to that of manufactured exports of the advanced economies has also accelerated and through 2007 had reached a trend of about 3 percent per year.

- A major factor underlying the increase in the demand for globally traded food crops has been the shift in the contribution to global growth of the emerging and developing countries. This source of increasing demand for food is likely to continue for some time.

- Increased interest on the part of global investors in holdings of commodity [that is, food and agriculture] futures contracts and mutual funds focused on commodities has contributed to the rise in the level of food prices recently. Although it may change inventory behavior, because this trading does not reduce the quantity of food available for consumption, it does not seem likely to be an important factor in raising the sustained trend in food prices.

• Agricultural production has been maintained over the past five years, but it has not increased to meet the rise in demand. As a consequence, stocks of the major food crops are down. Corn production devoted to use as ethanol accounts for much of the gains in supply of that crop.

• The most promising source of increased supply going forward to match the rising demand is increased yields in many of the world's agricultural producing countries.

Although the conclusion that global food prices are likely to continue to rise in relative and real terms cannot be unambiguously established, this analysis suggests that policy authorities should incorporate the risk of that outcome in their thinking. Changes in monetary, agriculture, and trade policy would follow accordingly.

Central banks, including the Fed, should manage future inflation risks by putting significant probability on the outcome that food prices continue to rise over the medium term. They should lessen the importance placed on the behavior of core measures of inflation and raise that placed on headline inflation while looking for new ways to distinguish "noise" from "signal" in that measure. Those central banks that still manage the exchange value of their currency, particularly those from large emerging market economies, should move to an exchange rate regime with greater flexibility.[2]

In light of current and prospective upward pressure on the relative price of food, policy officials should move away from measures that control and hence distort prices experienced by consumers and producers. If subsidies are continued, they should not be in the form of price supports. In particular, officials should avoid imposing arbitrary and nonmarket relative prices within the agricultural sector that influence supply decisions by producers. Officials should move away from land-use policies that were designed to manage surpluses. Policies that contribute to raising agricultural yields where those are subpar should be adopted. Efforts to improve the infrastructure in the agricultural sector should be enhanced.

Measures to restrict exports of agricultural products should be used only temporarily and as an emergency response to a critical problem. Over the medium term, such measures should be ended. Policies to liberalize market access for agricultural products should be adopted. Efforts to achieve success for the Doha Round should be strengthened.

Notes

1. Ethanol is a corn-based fuel.
2. Exchange rate refers to the relative value of a currency compared to other currencies.

Periodical and Internet Sources Bibliography

The following articles have been selected to supplement the diverse views presented in this chapter.

Kathy Chu	"Inflation in China May Help U.S. Exports," ABC. http://abcnews.go .com.
Raghav Gaiha and Nidhi Kaicker	"Does Food Inflation Hurt the Poor?," *Economic Times*, July 7, 2011. http://articles.economic times.indiatimes.com.
Rebecca Hellerstein	"The Impact of Inflation," Federal Reserve Bank of Boston, Winter 1997. www.bos.frb.org.
Anthony Mirhaydari	"Why Inflation Would Be Good for Us," MSN Money, April 13, 2010. http://articles.moneycentral .msn.com.
Sean O'Grady	"Soaring Inflation Hurts the Poor More, Says IFS," *Independent*, June 14, 2011. www.independent.co.uk.
Minxin Pai	"Inflation Scare Will Hurt China's Economy," *Financial Times*, November 18, 2010. www.ft.com.
Raj Patel	"That Witch, Inflation, Hurts Us More Without Protection," *Guardian*, January 18, 2011. www .guardian.co.uk.
David Pierson	"China Feels After-Effects of Economic Stimulus," *Los Angeles Times*, August 16, 2011. http:// articles.latimes.com.
Reuters	"With Inflation Low, Focus on Jobs: Fed's Rosengren," September 28, 2011. www.reuters.com.
Frank Shostak	"Does Inflation Promote Economic Growth or Does It Damage It?," BrookesNews.com, April 30, 2007. www.brookesnews.com.
Matthew Yglesias	"The Alternative to Deflation Is Inflation," ThinkProgress, March 27, 2011. http://thinkprogress.org.

CHAPTER 3

What Inflationary Conditions Pose the Greatest Threat to the US Economy?

Chapter Preface

Stagflation was an economic condition in the 1970s where inflation rose while unemployment fell. Hedge fund manager Douglass Kass argues for a new kind of economic condition related to stagflation: "screwflation."

In a June 11, 2011, article for *Barron's*, Kass says that screwflation "combines inflation with the screwing of the struggling middle class." Ian McAbeer at Seeking Alpha elaborates: "screwflation means the following: everything that you own is going down is value, meanwhile everything that you need to buy is going up in price."

Kass says that while the economy and corporate profits have expanded rapidly in the past thirty years, real wages in the United States have "made little recent progress" while "surging food and energy prices (among other cost pressures) now eat up middle-class incomes." Kass attributes screwflation to the globalization of the economy, which has sent many jobs overseas, and to advances in technology that have made many workers redundant. Whatever the cause, screwflation hurts the US economy as a whole. The middle class has less money to spend, which means that there is not enough demand to sustain an economic recovery, which means that jobs are cut.

Kass argues that screwflation could be brought under control by providing relief to the middle class. He suggests cutting taxes on the middle class and using tax incentives to encourage US businesses to create jobs in the United States rather than abroad. He also recommends using federal financing to reduce foreclosures for homeowners.

The viewpoints in the following chapter further discuss conditions that threaten the US economy, including hyperinflation, deflation, and stagflation.

| "Domestic economic stagnation will continue even though inflation is taking off."

The United States Is at Risk of Stagflation

Ronald McKinnon

Ronald McKinnon is a professor of economics at Stanford University. In the following viewpoint, he argues that the United States will experience stagflation—that is, high inflation and high unemployment. He says that the Federal Reserve's policy of low interest rates is the main contributor to stagflation. He argues that by pumping money into the economy, the Federal Reserve has destabilized developing economies that rely on the dollar and created runaway inflation. At the same time, he says that zero interest rates have made banks reluctant to lend, thus restricting growth.

As you read, consider the following questions:

1. What statistical evidence does McKinnon use in his argument that the economy is experiencing stagflation?

Ronald McKinnon, "The Return of Stagflation," *Wall Street Journal*, May 24, 2011. Reprinted from the *Wall Street Journal* © 2011 Dow Jones & Company. All rights reserved. Reproduced by permission of the author.

2. What are SMEs, and why does McKinnon say that they are important?
3. According to McKinnon, what caused the stagflation of the 1970s?

"Stagflation" is an ugly word for an ugly situation: persistent high inflation combined with high unemployment and stagnant demand in a country's economy. The term was coined by British politician Iain McLeod in a speech to Parliament in 1965. We haven't experienced it here in the United States since the bad old days of the 1970s.

Inflation and Unemployment

Yet with prices on the rise and unemployment still high, the U.S. economy again seems to be entering stagflation. April's [2011] producer price index for finished goods, which excludes services and falling home prices, rose 6.8%. The Bureau of Labor Statistics reports that intermediate goods prices for April were rising at a 9.4% annual clip. Meanwhile the official nationwide unemployment rate is mired close to 9%, without counting a large backlog of discouraged workers who are no longer officially in the labor force. So stagflation it is.

Although many forces buffet the U.S. economy, the near-zero interest rate [the cost of borrowing money] policy of the Federal Reserve is the prime contributor to the current bout with stagflation.

Since 1945, most of the world has been on a dollar standard. Today, for emerging markets outside of Europe, the dollar is used for invoicing both exports and imports; it is the intermediary currency used by banks for clearing international payments, and the intervention currency used by governments. To avoid conflict in targeting exchange rates,[1] the rule of the game is that the U.S. remains passive without an exchange-rate objective of its own.

Not having an exchange-rate constraint, the Fed can conduct a more independent monetary policy,[2] than other central banks can. How it chooses to exercise this independence is crucial to the stability of the international monetary system as a whole. For more than two years, the Fed has chosen to keep short-term interest rates on dollar assets close to zero and—over the past year—applied downward pressure on long rates through the so-called quantitative easing measures to increase purchases of Treasury bonds. The result has been a flood of hot money (i.e., volatile financial flows that are subject to reversals) from the New York financial markets into emerging markets on the dollar's periphery—particularly in Asia and Latin America, where natural rates of interest are much higher.

Inflation in Developing Economies

Wanting to avoid sharp appreciations of their currencies and losses in international competitiveness, many Asian and Latin American central banks intervened to buy dollars with domestic base monies and lost monetary control. This caused a surge in consumer price index (CPI) inflation of more than 5% in major emerging markets such as China, Brazil and Indonesia, with the dollar prices of primary commodities rising more than 40% world-wide over the past year. So the proximate cause of the rise in U.S. prices is inflation in emerging markets, but its true origin is in Washington.

There is a second, purely domestic avenue by which near-zero interest rates in U.S. interbank markets are constricting the economy. Since July 2008, the stock of so-called base money in the U.S. banking system has virtually tripled. As part of its rescue mission in the crisis and to drive interest rates down, the Fed has bought many nontraditional assets (e.g., mortgage-backed securities) as well as Treasurys [Treasury bonds]. Yet these drastic actions have not stimulated new bank lending. The huge increase in base money is now lodged as excess reserves in large commercial banks.

Stagflation in the 1970s

The 1970s are remembered as a decade of stagflation. Stocks fell about 15 percent in 1973, more than 25 percent in 1974. Unemployment hit 9 percent, while the official inflation rate climbed to 12.2 percent in 1974 and 13.3 percent in 1979. It was a period of confused monetary policy. Businesses encountered President Richard Nixon's disastrous wage and price controls, which fixed the prices at which they could sell, while they also had to contend with huge increases in borrowing costs. And then came the oil shocks. OPEC [Organization of the Petroleum Exporting Countries] warned repeatedly that a change in the value of the dollar would result in higher nominal oil prices, so when Nixon suspended dollar convertibility to gold in 1971, oil prices were bound to climb. They quadrupled from $3 per barrel in 1972 to $12 in 1974. They spiked again beginning in the late 1970s until they hit $35 in 1981.

Charles Goyotte, The Dollar Meltdown: Surviving the Coming Currency Crisis with Gold, Oil, and Other Unconventional Investments. *New York: Penguin, 2009.*

In mid-2011, the supply of ordinary bank credit to firms and households continues to fall from what it had been in mid-2008. Although large corporate enterprises again have access to bond and equity financing, bank credit is the principal source of finance for working capital for small and medium-sized enterprises (SMEs) enabling them to purchase labor and other supplies. In cyclical upswings, SMEs have traditionally been the main engines for increasing employment, but not in the very weak upswing of 2010–11, where employment gains have been meager or nonexistent.

Banks Are Broken

Why should zero interest rates be causing a credit constraint? After all, conventional thinking has it that the lower the interest rate the better credit can expand. But this is only true when interest rates—particularly interbank interest rates—are comfortably above zero. Banks with good retail lending opportunities typically lend by opening credit lines to nonbank customers. But these credit lines are open-ended in the sense that the commercial borrower can choose when—and by how much—he will actually draw on his credit line. This creates uncertainty for the bank in not knowing what its future cash positions will be. An illiquid bank could be in trouble if its customers simultaneously decided to draw down their credit lines.

If the retail bank has easy access to the wholesale interbank market, its liquidity is much improved. To cover unexpected liquidity shortfalls, it can borrow from banks with excess reserves with little or no credit checks. But if the prevailing interbank lending rate is close to zero (as it is now), then large banks with surplus reserves become loath to part with them for a derisory yield. And smaller banks, which collectively are the biggest lenders to SMEs, cannot easily bid for funds at an interest rate significantly above the prevailing interbank rate without inadvertently signaling that they might be in trouble. Indeed, counterparty risk in smaller banks remains substantial as almost 50 have failed so far this year.

That the American system of bank intermediation is essentially broken is reflected in the sharp fall in interbank lending: Interbank loans outstanding in March 2011 were only a third of their level in May 2008, just before the crisis hit. How to fix bank intermediation is a long story for another time. But it is clear that the Fed's zero interest-rate policy has worsened the situation. Without more lending to SMEs, domestic economic stagnation will continue even though inflation is taking off.

The stagflation of the 1970s was brought on by unduly easy U.S. monetary policy in conjunction with attempts to "talk" the dollar down, leading to massive outflows of hot money that destabilized the monetary systems of America's trading partners. Although today's stagflation is not identical, the similarities are striking.

Notes

1. Exchange rate is the rate at which one currency can be exchanged for another.
2. Monetary policy is the regulation of the amount of money in the economy.

"To date, there is no evidence that the wages of highly skilled workers are accelerating."

US Stagflation Fears Are Overblown

Oxford Analytica

Oxford Analytica is an independent strategic-consulting firm that draws on academic experts from Oxford University and elsewhere. In the following viewpoint, Oxford Analytica argues that the United States is not facing stagflation. It says there are signs of economic slowdown but few signs of inflationary pressures. Oxford Analytica also argues that some causes of stagflation in the past, such as strong unions and cost-of-living-adjustments to wages, are no longer as important a factor in the economy.

As you read, consider the following questions:

1. According to Oxford Analytica, what are examples of price shocks that some economists believe can boost underlying inflation?
2. The wage demands of which workers show inflationary trends first, according to Oxford Analytica?

3. What statistics does Oxford Analytica use to show that union membership has declined?

The combination of slowing growth and rising inflation has raised the specter of "stagflation," a pernicious problem in the U.S. in the 1970s and early 1980s. Stagflation is puzzling to economists because slowing growth should mean weakening demand for labor, lower wage inflation, and softer product demand. This, in turn, should mean falling inflation—not rising inflation.

1980 Precedent

The year 1980 epitomized the stagflation process. Real GDP fell by a sharp 1.6%, meaning that a serious recession was taking place. The unemployment rate jumped to 7% in 1980 from 5.8% the year before. Yet on top of this economic weakness, consumer price index (CPI) inflation accelerated to 13.5% from 11.3% the year before.

Recently, similar trends in the data have renewed U.S. stagflation fears:

- CPI inflation was 4% in February [2008]; the annualized rate of inflation was 4.7% over the previous six months— up from a 3.5% annual rate of inflation in the six months ending August 2007, and the 2.6% year-on-year rate of inflation as of December 2006.

- The unemployment rate has crept upward, from 4.5% in May 2007 to 4.8% in the last month.

- The pace of job creation has eased sharply from 175,000 net new jobs per month in 2006 to 107,000 jobs per month in the first half of 2007 to 76,000 jobs per month in the second half of 2007. In January and February of this year, an average of 43,000 jobs per month were lost.

- Meanwhile, commodity prices have soared. The price of gold has recently breached the $1,000-per-ounce mark—up from around $650 in January 2007. Oil prices have broken

$100 per barrel barrier and the Goldman Sachs commodity price index has recently surged to an all-time high.

Overblown Fears

Any assessment of the prospects for stagflation depends heavily on a theoretical understanding of the inflation process. Some economists believe that price shocks—like oil surges and rising food prices—can boost underlying inflation. However, most say that inflation spikes rarely become persistent if higher prices do not become embedded in workers' wages. Accepting this latter view, there are reasons to believe the current surge in inflation may be temporary.

Wages Contained

For all workers, total compensation was up 3% in the 12 months ending December 2007—less than the 3.1% increase in the 12 months ending September 2007.

Absent Danger Signal

The wage demands of the most technically sophisticated and skilled workers (those in management, professional and technical occupations) are a key indicator. When labor markets become tight and wage inflation starts to become a problem, it is the wages of these workers that show inflationary trends first, before the population at large.

To date, there is no evidence that the wages of highly skilled workers are accelerating. In the 12 months ending December 2007, total compensation for these workers was up 3.2%—less than the 3.4% increase experienced in the 12 months ending September 2007 or the 3.5% increase they enjoyed in the 12 months ending December 2006.

Productivity

Combined with the 1.6% annual productivity gains for the economy in 2007, these wage patterns suggest an underlying, annual "inflation impulse" into the U.S. economy of just 1.5% per year (roughly 3% wage gains, less 1.6% productivity gains).

Changed Labor Market

Another key difference between the current period and the late 1970s and early 1980s is that labor markets have changed dramatically:

- Union Decline. In the earlier period, unions represented approximately 20% of the labor force, and were often successful in pressing for higher wages, even in the face of slowing economic conditions. Just 12.1% of U.S. workers are currently members of unions, and union bargaining power has been significantly reduced.

- Few COLAs. A related factor is that cost-of-living adjustments (COLAs)[1] were a feature of labor markets in the late 1970s and early 1980s, when approximately 60% of union workers enjoyed COLA benefits. These COLA provisions made inflation difficult to combat, because it quickly worked its way into wages, which had subsequent effects on future inflation. Today, few workers have COLA clauses in their contracts, meaning that there are few automatic links between inflation and wages.

Note

1. COLAs automatically raise wages by the amount of inflation every year.

| "Today, too much supply is chasing too little demand."

The United States Is at Risk of Deflation

Mortimer B. Zuckerman

Mortimer B. Zuckerman is the chairman and editor-in-chief of US News & World Report. In the following viewpoint, he maintains that inflation is not a real risk for the US economy. He says that even though the Federal Reserve has flooded the economy with money, banks are still not lending and consumers are still not purchasing. Job creation, he says, is still weak, and seems likely to remain weak. Given these conditions, he argues, the real danger is falling prices, especially if the Federal Reserve decides to prematurely raise interest rates and tighten the money supply.

As you read, consider the following questions:

1. By how much does Zuckerman say that households, banks, and businesses will reduce their total debts in 2009?
2. According to Zuckerman, what is the output gap?
3. Why does Zuckerman say that inflation is easier to fix than deflation?

Is this the time to worry about inflation? We are, after all, awash in money with stagnant output.

No Borrowing

In the past year, the Federal Reserve has increased our monetary base by about 120 percent, more than double the previous highest annual increase over the past 50 years. The Fed has made huge loans to private lenders and bought over $1 trillion of mortgage securities and hundreds of billions of dollars of long-term treasury bonds. It has succeeded in lowering the federal funds rate [the interest rate at which banks can trade balances held at the Federal Reserve] below 1 percent—even, for most of the time, to less than half that. The goal, of course, is to force-feed money into the economy in the hope of sparking a recovery.

The mountain of reserves on bank balance sheets, which so scares the inflationary hawks, would normally encourage banks to lend and increase their profits. But while the Fed has been pumping money through the banks, little of it has entered the economic mainstream. Instead of boosting lending, the banks have just increased their reserves at the Fed by hundreds of billions of dollars.

The government may be borrowing more, but consumers and businesses are borrowing less. If anything, they are paying down their debts. Households will reduce their total debts by $200 billion this year [2009], Forbes magazine projects, and banks and businesses by $2.3 trillion. Small-business lending will contract by at least $113 billion. Since the credit crisis began more than two years ago [in 2007], credit available to consumers and the small-business sector—which employs half of the country's workforce—has contracted by trillions of dollars, mostly because of curtailment of credit card lines. The hope that new bank reserves would be available to prop up the faltering economy has not been fulfilled.

Inflation typically results from "too much money chasing too few goods." Today, too much supply is chasing too little demand.

*Inflation is bad, deflation is bad—
thank goodness for Carnation.*

Cartoon by Douglas Pike. www.CartoonStock.com.

That, coupled with consumers' need to save money to rebuild their finances, raises the risk of deflation, not inflation. As workers compete for scarce jobs and companies underbid one another for sales, both wages and prices will remain under pressure. We began this crisis with household debt at its highest levels since the 1930s. Knowing that monthly mortgage payments don't shrink even if your paycheck does, families are trying to deleverage and work down what they fear is their excessive debt. On top of that, households are suffering from substantial wealth losses tied to impaired equity portfolios and dropping home values. The combination of lower incomes and reduced wealth raises the likelihood that consumers will continue to boost their savings and pay down debt rather than spend more on consumption, which has put retail spending into one of its worst declines in decades. This is evidenced by retailers slashing inventories by record amounts, causing the percentage of capacity utilization in manufacturing to drop to the lowest reading in the 50-year history of the measure.

Demand growth would need to recover substantially to reverse the deflationary effects of low capacity utilization. For this, we would need a significant improvement in employment and hence spending. But the job market is even worse than the overall economy, and the prospect is that high levels of joblessness will persist beyond the end of the recession. Companies have cut the number of their employees and slashed other discretionary costs, such as advertising. This has significantly improved profit margins, even in the face of lower demand, but the higher profits are not coming from revenue growth but from lower costs, making it easier for companies to maintain or even cut prices rather than increase them.

The Recession Continues

Reduced spending by consumers and an extended high unemployment rate mean that we can look forward to a continuation of the output gap. This refers to the difference between the actual economic output and the most the economy could produce given the capital, know-how, and people available. That gap today is estimated to be between 8 and 10 percent, the largest on record. It makes for intense competition for scarce sales and jobs and results in continued downward pressure on prices.

It will take a long time to absorb the enormous slack of unused labor and production capacity created by the deepest recession since the 1930s—and it ain't really over yet. In the meantime, the labor market is showing a continuing decline in wages and in average hours worked per week (now down to 33 hours, the lowest in 60 years), suggesting it will be a long time before labor markets are strong enough to push up hourly wages and income.

Until employment grows enough to push wages, and income and production levels increase to more normal levels, the most pressing worry will be deflation, not inflation. This is evidenced by the financial markets. In 2007, according to Forbes.com, the Treasury Department issued $237 billion more in debt than it retired. This year [2009] just through October, it has added a stunning $1.2 trillion to its obligations, or $4 billion a day. With such a dramatic increase in supply to sell, you would think that prices would fall and yields would rise. Instead, after approaching 4 percent in June, yields on the 10-year treasury note have fallen steadily.

Despite worries that the government's huge deficit will create inflation and cause interest rates to spike, the bond market is signaling that its focus is on the dismal economy and the contraction of private-sector debt.

This does not mean we can forget about the long-term projected accumulation of debts and deficits. They can pose a danger. They can reignite inflation, especially if the quirky, unpredictably volatile "animal spirits" of entrepreneurs begin to break through. Foreigners may also become apprehensive about their purchases of too many dollar-denominated debt instruments, since they fear that the most politically acceptable way for the United States to handle its growing debts to other countries is through inflation. So far, though, we have still been able to export T-bills [Treasury bills] (even if we can't export goods) to finance our fiscal deficits.

Deflation Is More Dangerous than Inflation

In any event, inflation is easier to put right than deflation. The Federal Reserve can suppress inflation by raising interest rates as high as required to squelch those animal spirits, and the Fed can do that very rapidly. But there is a limit to the Fed's ability to confront deflation, since it cannot cut nominal rates below zero in order to induce economic growth. Therefore, risking inflation is a better bet than erring on the side of deflation.

Above all, we must avoid a repetition of an adverse feedback loop that would run from the declining real economy into the financial sector. While banks are broadly stabilized, they have yet to begin to operate as adequate lenders to U.S. households and corporations. That is why premature monetary tightening could push our economy into an even deeper decline.

Of course, when the economy really turns, monetary authorities must have the will to reverse policy quickly, tightening instead of easing. It is not something politicians like doing. Hence, they have been prone to running up huge and long-term fiscal deficits—deficits that, at some point, risk the financial stability and economic strength of America.

We cannot afford to let political leaders fudge and muddle along. We must find a way to mandate the appointment of strongly independent budget monitors who would be charged with the obligation to pass public judgment on the fiscal condition of our nation, in both the short and long terms and program by program. The Congressional Budget Office should be expanded to provide these cost and budget estimates, as it did for the healthcare debate. The CBO must be made even more independent and nonpartisan, with a regular obligation to make public its assessments. This is critical to prevent politicians from digging a bigger and bigger fiscal hole through deficit spending and the excessive accumulation of national debt in order to promote their re-election. That is the real danger emerging out of our present discontents.

"Over the past half-century in the US
... there hasn't been a single one-year
period when retail prices actually
declined. Not one."

Deflation Is Not a Serious Danger

Richard Salsman

Richard Salsman is president of InterMarket Forecasting Inc. in Durham, North Carolina. In the following viewpoint he argues that deflation is not a threat to the US economy. He says that the US economy has not experienced deflation in more than fifty years. Moreover, he says, periods of low inflation, or even deflation, are usually correlated with strong economic growth. In contrast, it is periods of inflation that correspond with weak growth. He says deflation fears are dangerous because they encourage the Federal Reserve to adopt inflationary policies that may hurt the economy.

As you read, consider the following questions:

1. How does Salsman define deflation and inflation?

2. What statistics does Salsman cite to show that the forty-four years between 1869 and 1913 were prosperous and deflationary?
3. Who faces genuine danger from deflation, according to Salsman?

Fears of "deflation" are widespread. By one account, "the scare word whispered around Washington these days is deflation, which means a falling price level and sometimes implies a stagnant if not collapsing economy." The "scare word" also spooks the U.S. Federal Reserve, which is now planning to print US$600-billion in more paper money, even though it has already tripled its balance sheet since 2008, and even though currency-gold prices, the world's most sensitive inflation indicators, have skyrocketed by 16% to 41% in the past year [2010] (depending on the currency), and by an average of 26%.

There Is No Deflation

In the past, gold-price jumps of such magnitude, which always mean a depreciation in the real purchasing power of paper money, i.e., inflation have been bearish [equities, or stocks, and growth, are falling] for equities and growth.

The current anxiety over "deflation," that is, an increase in money's purchasing power, causing a declining price level, is ridiculous, for two reasons: (1) there's no actual deflation to speak of (nor is it likely to occur in the coming few years, given prevailing public policies), and (2) even if some deflation were to take hold, it wouldn't necessarily be bearish for equities, profits or economic growth.

Deflation is an increase in the real purchasing power (or value) of money, i.e., an increase in what a certain sum of money can buy in terms of actual goods and services. This entails a decrease in the cost of living (and the cost of doing business), as reflected in a decline in the general level of prices and costs. In contrast, inflation is a decrease in the real purchasing power (or value) of money, i.e., a decrease in what money can buy in terms of actual goods and services. This entails an increase in the cost of living (and in the cost of doing business), as reflected in a rise in broad-based prices and costs.

Many economists presume, falsely, that deflation necessarily coincides with (or causes) a contraction in economic output. In fact, deflation by itself in no way curbs the motive to produce, because it doesn't preclude the maintenance of business profit margins. During the Industrial Revolution, deflation was common. It was also a bullish [it coincided with rising stocks and economic growth] phenomenon in the second half of the 19th century, the period of the fastest economic growth in human history. Consider the empirical record during the three to four decades between the U.S. Civil War (1861–65) and the First World War (1914–18). There was a huge increase in output (and profits) in the world's major economies during this period, even as price levels increased only marginally or even declined ("deflation").

Deflation and Growth

This was a period of widespread political-economic freedom. Contracts were respected, governments (and their debts) were minimal, taxes were low and money was sound [there was little inflation] (the classical gold standard lasted from 1870 to 1913). In the U.S. during these remarkable decades, there was no federal income tax, no central bank, no deposit insurance and no morass of regulatory agencies.

The table . . . shows how, despite stable or declining price levels, worldwide economic growth (real GDP) was quite rapid from 1880 to 1913 and inversely related to prices (with a negative correlation of -27%). Average annual "inflation" was only 0.3% in these nations from 1880 to 1913, while growth averaged 3.5% a year—a pairing that hasn't been matched in any 33-year period since.

This rebuts the myth that falling prices must coincide with a stagnating or contracting economy. Price levels declined in fast-growing nations such as Britain and Denmark, and increased only minimally amid robust economic growth rates elsewhere in the world. The "worst" inflation in 1880–1913 occurred in Portugal, so it suffered the second slowest rate of economic growth, but notice how its price level increased by just 22% in 33 years, an annual average inflation rate of only 0.7%. During these decades the U.S. price level increased only 10%, a mere 0.3% a year.

If we consult an even longer U.S. track record during the 44 years between 1869 and 1913, we find that real GDP skyrocketed by 461%, for an average growth rate of 10.5% a year, while the price level actually declined by 12%, or -0.3% a year.

Today's anxiety-ridden Keynesian economists[1] would have to concede that this was a long-term "deflation" in prices; worse (for them), they'd also have to admit what their theoretical "models" don't even permit them to conclude: that these deflationary decades coincided with stupendous rates of economic growth (indeed, sustained rates of high growth that haven't been matched since). The only subsequent, long-term stretch of robust U.S. growth occurred during the "Roaring Twenties," when the general price level declined yet again. From 1920 to 1929, real GDP in the U.S. expanded by 43% (or 4.7% a year), while the general price level declined by 17.7% (-2% a year). Profits and stock prices also zoomed during the decade. Again, deflation was no impediment to robust prosperity.

Deflation and the Depression

That deflation and economic depression seem to have coincided during the Great Depression of the 1930s has caused generations of economists to improperly indict (and fear) deflation. In fact, that debacle was instigated and prolonged not by "deflation" per se, but by a series of wealth-destroying public polices: (1) a deliberate inversion of the treasury yield curve by the Federal Reserve in 1928–29,[2] (2) huge tax hikes on a broad array of imports, starting in 1930 (the protectionist tariffs imposed by the Smoot-Hawley Act), (3) a massive hike in the federal income tax rate on the rich, from 25% in 1930 to 66% in 1932 (which slashed in half their incentive to produce income, since it cut the after-tax retention rate from 75% to 34%), and (4) a 41% devaluation of the U.S. dollar, in March 1933 (i.e., a one-time massive inflation).

By devaluing the dollar, the FDR [President Franklin Delano Roosevelt] regime made it worth less in real terms; it raised the gold price from US$20.7 per ounce to US$35, which reduced the dollar's gold content (real value) from roughly 1/21 of an ounce of gold to just 1/35 of an ounce of gold. This deliberate debasement in the dollar's real value, a value which had been steady over the prior four decades constituted inflation, not "deflation."

Although broad U.S. price indexes (and costs) declined sharply from 1930 to 1934, this was an effect of punitive public policies (yet another symptom), not itself a "cause" of the Great Depression. Punitive policies, each in their own perverse way, invited banks, business and the general public to hoard liquid and lower-risk assets, to raise their demand for cash balances, especially in the form of gold, due in large part to FDR's devaluation of the dollar, which boosted the gold price, and his threats to abandon the gold standard and seize private gold holdings. A rising demand for money, in the face of a declining supply of money (given bank failures and the extinction of chequing deposits, which comprise most of the money supply), necessarily raises the value of money (i.e., deflation), as reflected in falling prices.

As in the past, under the classical gold standard, businesses today could easily survive and even flourish under a mild, slowly drawn-out deflation, so long as their costs also declined and their profit margins were preserved. But the deflation of the early 1930s was quick and severe, leaving little scope for careful, rational adjustments in commercial-contractual relations among dislocated creditors and debtors.

Worse, the [President Herbert] Hoover-FDR regimes strong-armed businesses into not cutting their main cost—labour. Obtuse, Keynes-inspired policymakers in Washington insisted that consumers and labourers (not investors or businesses) drove

Price Level Change and Growth Under Gold Standard, 1880–1913

	Price Level	Real GDP
Britain	-10%	101%
Denmark	-8%	197%
France	2%	92%
Holland	6%	101%
Italy	7%	78%
US	10%	203%
Spain	11%	43%
Germany	15%	170%
Portugal	22%	56%

TAKEN FROM: Richard Salsman, "The Deflation Myth," *Financial Post*, January 27, 2011.

the economy, and, as such, they said wage rates and income levels shouldn't be allowed to fall but instead should be maintained at pre-1930 levels, even though this policy would necessarily sabotage profits, cause widespread losses and generate mass unemployment. The Keynesians certainly got what they asked for in the 1930s (not a recovery, but stagnation), yet instead of blaming themselves for the market carnage, they blamed "deflation"—the same phenomenon that, when mild and prolonged, was a direct boon to economic prosperity in 1880–1913 and 1920–29.

The only genuine danger from deflation is that faced by over-indebted, would-be deadbeats. When money gains value over time (as under deflation), the over-indebted face a larger repayment burden. They must repay their debt with ever more valuable money, compared with the (lesser) value of money initially borrowed. In a deflation, the prices (and incomes) one receives necessarily decline, but the face amount of the debt owed does not decline. This is the "pinch" that deflation ultimately exposes

and makes transparent. Joblessness only worsens the debt burden, but joblessness itself follows from excessively high real wage
rates (see the 1930s). The real danger (and difficulty) in economic
depression lies not in "deflation" per se, but in two fatal choices:
(1) to incur excessive debt (often made with the hope of repaying
in cheaper money, as under inflation), and (2) to demand excessive wage rates.

At root, unanticipated deflation really only hurts specula-
tors in leverage[3]—hardly the kind of people (or businesses) who
drive a genuinely productive and entrepreneurial economy. It is
creditors (i.e., savers, lenders and investors) who benefit from
deflation, all else being equal and so long as their clients aren't
over-leveraged. The so-called "fear of deflation" is nothing but
disguised sympathy for over-leveraged deadbeats[4] (or high-cost
firms), coupled with a thinly veiled disdain for greedy lenders,
bankers and investors.

It's not coincidental that in 1936 the Jack Kevorkian [a doctor who assisted in euthanasia]-sounding John Maynard Keynes
called for the "euthanasia of the rentier and, consequently, the
euthanasia of the cumulative oppressive power of the capitalist
to exploit the scarcity value of capital." In 2009 the [President
Barack] Obama government jettisoned the U.S. Bankruptcy
Code so as to cheat the bondholders of General Motors and
Chrysler, and favour the United Auto Workers. The "rentier"
is the presumed dastardly bondholder who lives on his earned
interest.

In any case, deflation is currently hardly a risk. Over the past
half-century in the U.S. (July 1960 to July 2010), there hasn't
been a single one-year period when retail prices actually declined. Not one.

Low Inflation Does Not Lead to Deflation

The U.S. retail-price inflation rate has been relatively low lately,
especially compared with the double-digit inflation rates of

1975–82. But does that mean today's low inflation rate is poised to move lower still, until it tips "inevitably" into the deflationary zone? Not necessarily, especially since at no time in the past 50 years did a U.S. inflation rate ever tumble into a deflation rate. There's been no annual deflation in the U.S. since 1960, only different rates of inflation—periods of faster rising or slower rising prices.

The U.S. economy has had a declining rate of inflation in the past year, but history says that's good for economic recoveries and expansions. The thing to have feared in the past few years was accelerating rates of inflation, as in 2006–08, since that signalled trouble for the economy, profits and stocks.

But investors never hear much from printing-press Keynesians about the potential dangers of a rising inflation rate. All they seem to hear about is whining and worrying about the alleged dangers of deflation. This Keynesian media bias tends to prompt Fed policymakers into taking actions and adopting quantitative easing [a means of increasing the money in the economy] schemes that threaten to boost the inflation rate—the real menace.

Notes

1. John Maynard Keynes was an influential economist who argued that high interest rates and low inflation can hurt economic growth.
2. Under normal circumstances, treasury bonds held for longer periods yield greater returns. In 1928–1929, this flipped, so bonds held for shorter periods yielded greater returns.
3. Leverage usually means borrowing money to invest.
4. To be overleveraged means to have borrowed too heavily.

"From there the scenario plays out as it has elsewhere: panic, food shortages, riots, martial law."

The United States Is at Risk of Hyperinflation

Bob Adelmann

Bob Adelmann is a former businessman and libertarian journalist who writes for New American. *In the following viewpoint, he argues that hyperinflation is a dangerous and destructive force. He says that hyperinflation wreaks havoc on the economy and causes a loss of faith in government, which can result in anarchy and authoritarianism. Adelmann argues that the actions of the Federal Reserve may result in hyperinflation and he suggests eliminating the Federal Reserve.*

As you read, consider the following questions:

1. What does Adelmann say is perhaps the most famous hyperinflation of all time?
2. According to Adelmann, what was the trigger event that caused German hyperinflation?

3. According to James Wesley Rawles, what citizens would be wiped out within two weeks by hyper-inflation?

David Galland's article for the *Daily Reckoning* painted a picture of imminent collapse [as of October 2011] of America's monetary system, which was followed four days later by Clive Maund's possible scenario of bank failures following on the heels of a eurozone collapse. Mamta Badkar raised the specter of hyperinflation in his *Business Insider* article by reviewing the "10 Worst Hyper-Inflation Horror-Stories of the Past Century," reflecting interest in whether, or how, the economic disaster of hyperinflation would affect the United States.

Past Hyperinflation

According to Badkar, the runaway inflation of Germany in the early 1920s is one of the worst cases in history, where, at its nadir, the monthly inflation rate reached 29,500 percent in October 1923. In post-World War II Greece, inflation peaked at 20.9 percent a month in October 1944, while in July 1946, inflation in Hungary hit 207 percent daily. In China, following the Second World War, inflation reached 2,178 percent in May 1949, equivalent to a daily rate of 11 percent.

In the mid-1970s, Chile suffered from an inflation rate of 746 percent annually, while Argentina's inflation rate in 1989 hit 12,000 percent. Bolivia's inflation between May and August 1985 hit 60,000 percent on an annual basis. Nicaragua's inflation rate in 1987 exceeded 30,000 percent; Yugoslavia's daily rate of inflation reached 64.6 percent between 1989 and 1994; and in perhaps the most famous hyperinflation of all time, the purchasing power of Zimbabwean dollars was virtually obliterated, with inflation reaching 416 quintillion percent annually.

German citizens related their stories of how they were impacted. Walter Levy, a German-born oil consultant in New York, commented:

Highest Monthly Inflation Rates in History

Country	Month with highest inflation rate	Highest monthly inflation rate	Equivalent daily inflation rate	Time required for prices to double
Hungary	July 1946	1.30×10^{16}%	195%	15.6 hours
Zimbabwe	Mid-November 2008 (latest measurable)	79,600,000,000%	98.0%	24.7 hours
Yugoslavia	January 1994	313,000,000%	64.6%	1.4 days
Germany	October 1923	29,500%	20.9%	3.7 days
Greece	November 1944	11,300%	17.1%	4.5 days
China	May 1949	4,210%	13.4%	5.6 days

TAKEN FROM: Steve H. Hanke, "R.I.P. Zimbabwe Dollar," Cato Institute, May 3, 2010. www.cato.org/zimbabwe.

My father was a lawyer and he had taken out an insurance policy in 1903, and every month he had made the payments faithfully. It was a 20-year policy, and when it came due, he cashed it in and bought a single loaf of bread.

A student at Freiburg University ordered a cup of coffee at a café. The price on the menu was 5,000 marks. He had two cups. When the bill came, it was for 14,000 marks. When he complained, he was told, "If you want to save money, and you want two cups of coffee, you should order them both at the same time."

A German factory worker described payday, which was every day:

At 11:00 in the morning a siren sounded, and everybody gathered in the factory forecourt, where a five-ton lorry was drawn up loaded brimful with paper money. The chief cashier and his assistants climbed up on top. They read out our names and just threw out bundles of notes. As soon as you had caught one you made a dash for the nearest shop and bought just anything that was going.

Hyperinflation in the United States

Notably missing from Badkar's summary was any mention of hyperinflation in the United States and yet, as explained by Charles Scaliger in *The New American*, for nearly 100 years prior to the Constitutional Convention in 1787, the infant society suffered repeatedly from the disasters and aftereffects of government printing of paper money without commodity backing to pay its bills. Such printing, Scaliger noted, "has the potential to damage severely the body politic. Hyperinflation in particular is usually accompanied by civil unrest, regime change, and dictatorship. Wherever it rears its ugly head, confidence in banks, money, and the economy as a whole is lost. Savings are wiped out as currencies lose value, and pauperized citizens revert to a barter economy." Scaliger noted that all it takes is a "trigger" to start the hyperinflationary process sufficient to cause "not merely a currency correction but a calamitous collapse of the entire economy on a scale that would dwarf even the hyperinflation of the Revolutionary War."

In the confidence model of hyperinflation, all it takes is "some event, or series of events, [to] remove the belief that the authority issuing the money will remain solvent."

For Germany that "trigger" event was the assassination of a well-known politician, Walter Rathenau. As noted by George Goodman in *Paper Money*, "Rathenau was a charismatic figure, and the idea that a popular, wealthy and glamorous government minister could be shot in a law-abiding society shattered the faith of the Germans, who wanted to believe that things were going to be all right. Rathenau's state funeral was a national trauma." The unraveling of the German economy began soon thereafter as people, having lost faith in the government, also lost faith in their currency.

In a plausible scenario, Gonzalo Lira, writing for the *Business Insider*, proposed how a "trigger" event could begin the unraveling in the United States [as the actions of the Federal Reserve trigger a panic sell off of treasury bonds]. . . .

He concludes his plausible scenario:

> By the end of that terrible day, commodities of all stripes—precious and industrial metals, oil, foodstuffs—will shoot the moon. But it will not be because ordinary citizens have lost faith in the dollar (that will happen in the days and weeks ahead)—it will happen because once Treasuries are [no longer] the sure store of value, where are all those money managers supposed to stick all those dollars? By the end of the day of this panic, commodities will have risen between 50% and 100%. By week's end, we're talking 150% to 250%. Of course, once commodities start to balloon, that's when the ordinary citizens will get their first taste of hyperinflation. They'll see it at the gas pumps.

From there the scenario plays out as it has elsewhere: panic, food shortages, riots, martial law.

End the Fed

In his book *Patriots*, author James Wesley Rawles notes that in this scenario, Washington and the Federal Reserve are virtually powerless to stop the hyperinflation: "All that the bureaucrats in Washington, D.C. could do was watch it happen. They had sown the seeds decades before when they started deficit spending. Now they were reaping the whirlwind:"

> Citizens on fixed incomes were wiped out financially by the hyperinflation within two weeks. These included pensioners, those on unemployment insurance, and welfare recipients. Few could afford to buy a can of beans when it cost $150. The riots started soon after inflation bolted past the 1,000 percent mark. Detroit, New York and Los Angeles were the first cities to see full-scale rioting and looting. Soon, the riots engulfed most other large cities.

It doesn't have to happen. With sufficient understanding, citizens will not only recognize the nearness of the peril but their ability to impress upon their representatives the proper course to take: Stop the spending and end the Fed.

| "But does this mean that inflation may evolve into a hyperinflation in the US? I believe not."

Hyperinflation Is Not a Serious Danger

Peter Bernholz

Peter Bernholz is professor emeritus at Basel University in Switzerland. In the following viewpoint, he says that the Federal Reserve has pumped large amounts of money into the economy in response to the financial crisis of 2008–2009. Bernholz argues that the Fed's expansionary policy may lead to another speculative bubble and another recession when the bubble bursts. However, he says, the Fed is not directly engaged in money creation, and foreign governments hold a great deal of US currency. As a result of these factors, Bernholz says that the Fed's actions will probably not result in hyperinflation.

As you read, consider the following questions:

1. Name three defects in the financial system according to Bernholz.
2. By how much does Bernholz say the US deficit rose from 2007 to 2009?

Peter Bernholz, "How Likely Is Hyperinflation?," *American*, December 15, 2009. All rights reserved. Reproduced by permission.

3. Which countries does Bernholz say have incredibly huge holdings of dollar bills?

During the past several months, concerns have risen that the expansionary policies [expanding the money supply] of the U.S. government and the Federal Reserve System to counter the present crisis [the financial crisis of 2008–2009] are creating the danger of a substantial future inflation. Some speak even of a hyperinflation, that is, of a rate of inflation exceeding 50 percent per month. People believing in the latter scenario base their concerns on results I presented in *Monetary Regimes and Inflation: History, Economic and Political Relationships*, which shows that all hyperinflations were caused by huge government deficits. By analyzing many historical examples, I illustrated how hyperinflations resulted whenever 40 percent or more of government expenditures were financed by money creation. Since it is expected that about 42 percent of U.S. expenditures will be financed by credits this year, some fear the emergence of hyperinflation in the United States. Consequently we face the interesting question of whether a very high U.S. inflation with a corresponding fall of exchange rates has to be expected.

Bubbles and Financial Weakness

In discussing this question, let me state two facts which in my view cannot be denied: First, that the present crisis has been initiated by the Federal Reserve's too expansionary monetary policies after the bursting of the New Economy Bubble.[1] Second, that the Fed and the U.S. government embarked on even more expansionary policies to fight the present crisis; indeed, their policies constitute an experiment on a scale which has never been seen before in the history of fighting crises.

Let me turn to the first point. In a mistaken fear of deflation, the Fed lowered its interest rate to 1 percent and increased the monetary base by about 39 percent from 2000 to 2006 after the bursting of the New Economy Bubble. In doing so it encouraged an incredible credit expansion by the financial sector and thus allowed the subsequent asset bubble.[2] Later, it helped to pierce the bubble by raising its interest rate step by step above 5 percent and by strongly reducing the growth of the monetary base. Though the Fed thus initiated the crisis, we should not forget that it would never have taken such a dramatic course, which hurt the real economy, were there not other well-known defects in the financial system such as:

- Banks neglected to maintain a sufficiently diversified portfolio.
- The compensation systems for leading managers were based far too much on short-term performances.
- The control system within banks failed.
- Rating agencies financed by their customers grossly misjudged the values of firms and assets.
- The measures by the U.S. government to ease the buying of houses by relatively poor people proved mistaken.
- American liability rules in case owners could not pay the interest on their mortgages encouraged levels of indebtedness that were too high.
- The liability rules for gross mistakes by leading managers of business firms were too restricted.
- The percentages of own capital required for banks by internationally agreed rules (Basel II) [an international agreement on banking rules] and the valuation at market prices adhered to during the crisis exacerbated it.
- The permission by Basel II for banks to employ their own models to evaluate risks was a mistake.
- The control of financial institutions by government agencies failed.
- The lack of knowledge of economic history by leading managers encouraged them to take overly risky decisions.

Before taking up the second point, namely the possible consequences of measures taken by Fed and U.S. government to counter the crisis, let me stress that crises cannot be prevented in a decentralized and innovative market economy. It may be possible to mitigate them by adequate reforms or even to prevent one or the other. But that is the best result one can hope for.

This can be demonstrated by looking at crises from two different perspectives. By analyzing historical events, Charles Kindleberger has shown in *Manias, Panics and Crashes* that 29 financial crises occurred from 1720 to 1975. This means that, on average, each decade experiences an unpredictable crisis, though very strong crises are rather rare. For instance, besides the 1929 crisis, another in 1873 was severe, lasting about six to seven years and hitting the real economy from Europe to the United States, Argentina, and Australia. Apart from the historical evidence for the inevitability of crises, mathematical chaos theory has demonstrated that systems characterized by non-linear feedbacks[3] can be hit by unpredictable fluctuations. And a decentralized market economy has quite a number of such feedbacks—for instance, changing expectations of consumers and producers, fluctuations in the volume of net investments, governmental interventions, central bank policies, and the reaction of prices to unpredictable innovations.

A Danger of Hyperinflation?

Let us turn now to the second point, whether grave dangers loom because of the measures taken by central banks and governments to fight the present crisis. Is there even a danger of hyperinflation in the United States? Let us first consider the facts. Central banks led by the Fed have indeed lowered their interest rates to nearly zero percent. The monetary base of the Fed has grown by about 99 percent within one year from the end of July 2008, and this following a substantial increase already since the end of 2008. Even the Swiss National Bank increased its monetary base by 112.5 percent from the end of 2008 to the end of

May of 2009. The growth of the monetary base in the euro zone looks more modest, with 68 percent since the end of 2007. But even this smaller increase has never been experienced in monetary history except in countries suffering from high inflation.

Government finances, too, have worsened dramatically because of the measures taken to fight the crisis. The U.S. deficit rose from 2.9 percent of Gross Domestic Product (GDP) in 2007 to 8 percent in the fourth quarter of 2008; for 2009 a deficit of 10.2 percent is expected. This implies that the indebtedness of the United States will reach 73.2 percent of GDP in this year. In Great Britain the deficit grew from 2.7 percent to 5.4 percent in 2008, whereas one of 9.3 percent is foreseen for 2009. In the euro zone, the deficit of member states increased from 3.5 percent in the fourth quarter of 2007 to 9.3 percent of GDP by the end of 2008.

But were these measures not justified because of the dramatic situation and the dangers threatening in the crisis? It is difficult to form a judgement because of the extraordinary extent of the measures and because we do not know the further course of the crisis. Certainly some steps like those taken to save General Motors were not warranted [in December 2008 the US government made loans to GM to prevent bankruptcy]. But even if all the measures may help mitigate and shorten the crisis, which is probable, it has to be asked whether lowering interest rates and expanding the monetary base—measures similar to those which have already initiated the present crisis—will not bring about even worse developments in the future.

Speaking to members of the board of central banks, one is assured that they are technically able to reduce the enlarged monetary base and to increase their interest rates to normal levels any time. This is probably true. Asking, however, whether they will be able to do so given the political and psychological pressures to be expected when timely measures to prevent inflation by rising interest rates have to be taken, the answer is again "yes." But this seems to be rather doubtful since such adjustments would have to be made at a time when tender growth has just set in and when unemployment may still be rising. A stiffening of monetary policies to fight inflation needs about two years before results can be observed. It is thus not surprising that former board members of central banks and well-informed economists are much more skeptical concerning the chances of increasing interest rates and reducing the monetary base in time.

Bad Consequences

It is thus probable that in the future we will have to face a mistaken policy's bad consequences. But what are the fundamental mistakes of this policy? To understand the underlying problems we have to remember a mostly forgotten important function of financial institutions in a decentralized market economy. In such a system it is one of their tasks to coordinate the savings of consumers (including obligatory ones for health and unemployment insurance) with the net investment of non-financial business firms and governments. In real terms this corresponds to a reallocation of factors of production from producing consumer goods to the production of means of production with the consequence that more and new goods can be produced in the future. Savings by consumers transferred as additional means to producers lead to a reduction in the demand for consumption goods and allow productive firms to increase their investments.

In this process the real interest rate is determined by the impatience to consume and the greater productivity of more roundabout production processes (or expressed otherwise, the marginal productivity of real capital). The resulting "natural" real rate of interest can change to a minor degree, but should, judging from the non-inflationary environment of the gold standard in developed countries before 1914, be around 3 to 4 percent. This means that if central banks lower the nominal rate of interest below the natural rate, they send the wrong signal to producers, including builders and purchasers of houses. They are motivated to indebt themselves to initiate additional investments and to

145

enter production processes which would be unprofitable at interest rates from 3 to 4 percent. Consequently, not all of these investment decisions can be executed since not enough real factors of production are put at their disposal by the real savings of households.

In real terms, net investment must always equal savings. As a consequence, there remain only two ways to bring this equality about if nominal interest rates are too low and are disturbing this relationship. Either the central bank increases interest rates again—in this case, the net investments initiated are no longer profitable and have to be interrupted, as happened with the housing crisis in the United States—or the central bank leaves interest rates at their too low level, resulting in inflationary developments that cannot be avoided. The use of means of production for goods consumed by households is forcibly reduced since the purchasing power of their incomes and the value of their nominal assets are reduced. In both ways, or by some intermediate combination of them, the equality of savings and net investments is restored.

Measures taken by monetary and fiscal policies neglecting these real relationships are bound to fail, as already stressed by the Swedish economist Knut Wicksell in his *Geldzins und Gueterpreise* (*Interest and Prices*) in 1898. This means that central banks and especially the Fed are now confronted by a huge dilemma—huge because of the very dimension of financial support unknown in history, as illustrated by the figures presented [in the table]. And this dilemma is increased by the fact that high budget deficits of governments have to be financed. If expectations of households and firms become positive, another sizable asset bubble has to be expected because of the vast liquidity created. And inflation will follow the bubble if the Fed does not act speedily and strongly to reduce the monetary base and to increase the interest rate to normal levels. But such a policy may lead to another crisis and recession. On the other hand, if the Fed does act too late and not strongly enough, inflation cannot be prevented.

An escape from this dilemma seems only to be possible if the change to positive expectations and the rise of production follows a slow and continuous development, so that enough time is available to slowly increase interest rates and slowly reduce the monetary base and government budget deficits. But this path is not available in case of a rapid recovery. For then the danger of a sizable inflation is a real one.

No Hyperinflation

But does this mean that inflation may evolve into a hyperinflation in the United States? I believe not. Though it is true that budget deficits with government expenditures covered by 40 percent or more through credits have historically led to hyperinflation, it has been stressed [in Bernholz's book] *Monetary Regimes and Inflation* that it is not only the size of these credits but also their composition that is important. This is noted in the book thus: "It will be demonstrated by looking at 12 hyperinflations that they have all been caused by the financing of huge budget deficits through money creation". This expresses the fact that only credit extended directly or indirectly by the monetary authorities to the government leads to the creation of money, that is, an increase of the monetary base. This is not true for borrowings taken up in the capital markets if they are not resold to the Fed. Looking from this perspective at the U.S. deficit, by far not all of the credits borrowed by the government were financed by the Fed. According to preliminary and rough estimates, not 40 percent but "only" about 13 percent of U.S. expenditures are presently financed this way. Moreover, in discussing this problem it has to be taken into account that about two-thirds of dollar bills are estimated to circulate abroad. This—together with the fact that incredibly huge holdings of dollar assets are owned especially by the central banks of China, India, and the Gulf States—may pose other and later dangers. But these dangers will be, except for a return of the dollar bills and a purchase of foreign-owned dollar assets by the Fed, of a different nature. Inflation may rise more or less strongly during the next years, but there is presently no danger of a hyperinflation in the United States.

Notes

1. The New Economy Bubble, or Dot com bubble, was a stock market bubble that resulted when Internet stocks were overvalued between 1995 and 2000.
2. In the second half of the 2000s, housing prices became extremely overvalued.
3. Nonlinear feedback means that actions taken create results that feed back to multiply the results.

Periodical and Internet Sources Bibliography

The following articles have been selected to supplement the diverse views presented in this chapter.

Thomas J. Feeney

"The Danger of Hyperinflation," *Seeking Alpha*, December 24, 2010. http://seekingalpha.com.

Simon Johnson

"An Overblown Fear," *New York Times*, May 23, 2011. www.nytimes .com.

Kathleen Madigan

"Without Wage Pressures, Stagflation Fears Are Overblown," *Wall Street Journal*, April 29, 2011. http://blogs.wsj.com.

Ronald McKinnon

"The Return of Stagflation," *Wall Street Journal*, May 24, 2011. http:// online.wsj.com.

Panos Mourdoukoutas

"China Is Heading for Stagflation," *Forbes*, December 4, 2011. http:// online.wsj.com.

Hamilton Nolan

"Attention, Tea Party: Deflation Is Coming," *Gawker*, August 2, 2010. http://gawker.com.

Adam S. Posen

"Not That '70s Show: Why Stagflation Is Unlikely," Peterson Institute for International Economics, June 27, 2011. www .iie.com/publications/papers/po sen20110627.pdf.

Cullen Roche

"The Truth About Hyperinflation: It's More Than Just a Monetary Phenomena," *Business Insider*, March 21, 2011. http://articles .businessinsider.com.

Karl Smith

"How Can the Fed Avoid Hyper-Inflation?," *Modeled Behavior*, September 9, 2011. http://mod eledbehavior.com.

Paul Toscano

"The Worst Hyperinflation Situations of All Time," CNBC, February 14, 2011. www.cnbc.com.

For Further Discussion

Chapter 1

1. Howard Baetjer Jr. argues that oil prices sometimes rise because of demand, but that that does not constitute inflation. Inflation, he says, is a rise in overall prices. Would John Kemp agree with this analysis? Why or why not? Does Kemp think that there is a single rate of inflation?

2. Steve Saville says that one of the "primary job requirements" of the central bank is "to deceive." What does Saville believe the central bank is deceiving people about? Would John T. Harvey agree? Explain your answer.

Chapter 2

1. What bad effects does Brad Lyle say inflation has on the economy? What positive effects can inflation have, according to Ha-Joon Chang? Provide one piece of evidence that each uses to support his position. Who do you think makes the more convincing case?

2. The *Economist* argues that inflation causes more consumption, which might be a good thing for China, where consumption is low. Why are people more likely to spend when there is inflation? (Hint: If car prices are rising quickly, does it make sense to save up for a car or to buy it now?) Would you expect deflation (a fall in prices) to increase or decrease consumer spending? Why?

Chapter 3

1. Richard Salsman says that only "over-indebted, would-be deadbeats" face danger from deflation. Is this language neutral or prejudicial? Would you agree that people hurt by falling house prices in the last few years are "would-be deadbeats"? Explain your answer.

2. Bob Adelmann argues that all that is needed to start hyper-inflation is a "trigger" event which will cause people to lose faith in the solvency, or financial stability of the government. Does Peter Bernholz think that this is how hyperinflation starts? What factors does Bernholz suggest lead to hyperinflation?

Organizations to Contact

The editors have compiled the following list of organizations concerned with the issues debated in this book. The descriptions are derived from materials provided by the organizations. All have publications or information available for interested readers. The list was compiled on the date of publication of the present volume; names, addresses, phone and fax numbers, and e-mail and Internet addresses may change. Be aware that many organizations take several weeks or longer to respond to inquiries, so allow as much time as possible.

The American Enterprise Institute (AEI)
1150 Seventeenth Street NW
Washington, DC 20036
(202) 862-5800 • fax: (202) 862-7177
e-mail: webmaster@aei.org
website: www.aei.org

The American Enterprise Institute for Public Policy Research is a privately funded organization dedicated to research and education on issues of government, politics, economics, and social welfare. Its purposes are to defend the principles and improve the institutions of American freedom and democratic capitalism, including limited government and private enterprise. AEI publishes books such as *Privatizing Fannie Mae, Freddie Mac,* and the *Federal Home Loan Banks*, and its website includes numerous articles and policy papers on economic issues.

Board of Governors of the Federal Reserve System
20th Street and Constitution Avenue NW
Washington, DC 20551
(202) 452-3000
website: www.federalreserve.gov

The Federal Reserve System is the central bank of the United States. It was founded by Congress in 1913 to provide the nation with a safer, more flexible, and more stable monetary and financial system. It produces publications for specialists such as *International Journal of Central Banking* as well as consumer-oriented publications such as *Consumer's Guide to Mortgage Refinancing.*

Bretton Woods Committee (BWC)
1990 M Street NW, Suite 450
Washington, DC 20036
(202) 331-1616 • fax: (202) 785-9423
e-mail: info@brettonwoods.org
website: www.brettonwoods.org

BWC is a bipartisan group dedicated to increasing public understanding of international financial and development issues and the role of the World Bank, International Monetary Fund, and World Trade Organization. Members include industry and financial leaders, economists, university leaders, and former government officials. On its website, BWC publishes the quarterly *BWC Newsletter* and numerous policy papers and reports.

The Brookings Institution
1775 Massachusetts Avenue NW
Washington, DC 20036
(202) 797-6000 • fax: (202) 797-6004
e-mail: communications@brookings.edu
website: www.brookings.edu

The Brookings Institution is a private nonprofit organization devoted to conducting independent research, including economy research, and developing innovative policy solutions. Brookings' goal is to provide high-quality analysis and recommendations for decision-makers on the full range of challenges facing an increasingly interdependent world. The Brookings Institution publishes books on economic matters such as *Budgeting for Hard Power* as well as numerous policy papers and reports available through its website.

The Cato Institute
1000 Massachusetts Avenue NW
Washington, DC 20001-5403
(202) 842-0200 • fax: (202) 842-3490
e-mail: webmaster@cato.org
website: www.cato.org

The Cato Institute conducts research on public policy issues in order to promote consideration of traditional American principles of limited government, individual liberty, free markets and peace. It publishes reviews and journals such as *Economic Freedom of the World* and *Cato Journal* as well as policy papers and opinion pieces.

Center for American Progress
1333 H Street NW, 10th Floor
Washington, DC 2005
(202) 682-1611
e-mail: progress@americanprogress.org
website: www.americanprogress.org

The Center for American Progress is a progressive think tank with an interest in values like diversity, shared and personal responsibility, and participatory government. It publishes broadly on economic issues including business regulation, credit and debt, the global economy, health care, immigration, and the environment.

Competitive Enterprise Institute (CEI)
1899 L Street NW, 12th Floor
Washington, DC 20036
(202) 331-1010 • fax: (202) 331-0640
e-mail: info@cei.org
website: www.cei.org

CEI is a nonprofit public policy organization dedicated to advancing the principles of free enterprise and limited government. It believes that individuals are best helped not by government intervention but by making their own choices in a free marketplace. CEI's publications include the monthly newsletter *CEI Planet* and articles such as "Stimulate the Economy Through Deregulation."

The Economic Policy Institute
1333 H Street NW, Suite 300, East Tower
Washington, DC 20005
(202) 775-8810 • fax: (202) 775-0819
e-mail: researchdept@epi.org
website: www.epi.org

The Economic Policy Institute is a nonprofit, nonpartisan think tank that seeks to broaden the public debate about strategies to achieve a prosperous and fair economy. The Economic Indicators page on the EPI website includes current information on US GDP, family income, international trade and investment, jobs, and wages. Issues Guides are provided on living wage, minimum wage, offshoring, poverty and family budgets, retirement security, social security, unemployment insurance, and welfare.

European Commission—Economic and Financial Affairs (ECOFIN)
Unit R 4, B-1049
Brussels, Belgium
fax: 32 (0)2 298 09 98
website: http://ec.europa.eu

ECOFIN is entrusted with the regulation of European Union economic and monetary policy. Its goal is to ensure the smooth functioning of economic integration in the EU. Its website includes access to news articles on the European economic situation and links to its electronic publications such as *European*

Economy News, European Economy Research Letter, economics forecasts, and research papers.

The Heritage Foundation
214 Massachusetts Avenue NE
Washington, DC 20002-4999
(202) 546-4400 • fax (202) 546-8328
e-mail: info@heritage.org
website: www.heritage.org

The Heritage Foundation is a research and educational institute that promotes conservative public policies based on the principles of free enterprise, limited government, individual freedom, traditional American values, and a strong national defense. Its website includes policy briefs on US agriculture, the economy, health care, the federal budget and spending, labor, retirement and social security, as well as international trade policy and economic freedom.

International Monetary Fund (IMF)
700 19th Street NW
Washington, DC 20431
(202) 623-7000 • fax: (202) 623-4661
e-mail: publicaffairs@imf.org
website: www.imf.org

IMF is an international organization of 184 member countries. It was established to promote international monetary cooperation, exchange stability, and orderly exchange arrangements. IMF fosters economic growth and high levels of employment and provides temporary financial assistance to countries. It publishes the quarterly *Finance & Development* and reports on its activities, including the quarterly *Global Financial Stability Report,* recent issues of which are available on its website along with data on IMF finances and individual country reports.

Ludwig von Mises Institute
518 West Magnolia Avenue

Auburn, Alabama 36832-4501
(334) 321-2100 • fax: (334) 321-2119
e-mail: contact@mises.org
website: http://mises.org

The Ludwig von Mises Institute is a research and educational center devoted to libertarian politics and the Austrian School of economics (which is strongly opposed to loose money policies and inflation). The Mises Institute provides educational materials, conferences, media, and literature to educate the public about the importance of the market economy and sound money, and the dangers of government intervention.

Bibliography of Books

Ben S. Bernanke, Thomas Laubach, Frederic S. Mishkin, and Adam S. Posen

Inflation Targeting: Lessons from the International Experience. Princeton, NJ: Princeton University Press, 2001.

Peter Bernholz

Monetary Regimes and Inflation: History, Economic and Political Relationships. Cheltenham, UK: Edward Elgar, 2006.

Peter Clarke

Keynes: The Rise, Fall, and Return of the 20th Century's Most Influential Economist. New York, NY: Bloomsbury Press, 2009.

Tyler Cowen

The Great Stagnation: How America Ate All the Low-Hanging Fruit of Modern History, Got Sick, and Will (Eventually) Feel Better. New York: Dutton Adult, 2011.

Chris Farrell

Deflation: What Happens When Prices Fall. New York: HarperCollins, 2004.

Adam Ferguson

When Money Dies: The Nightmare of Deficit Spending, Devaluation, and Hyperinflation in Weimar Germany. New York: PublicAffairs, 2010.

Ethan S. Harris	*Ben Bernanke's Fed: The Federal Reserve After Greenspan.* Boston, MA: Harvard Business School Publishing, 2008.
Joshua Holland	*The Fifteen Biggest Lies About the Economy: And Everything Else the Right Doesn't Want You to Know About Taxes, Jobs, and Corporate America.* Hoboken, NJ: John Wiley & Sons, 2010.
Greg Ip	*The Little Book of Economics: How the Economy Works in the Real World.* Hoboken, NJ: John Wiley & Sons, 2010.
Zachary Karabell	*Superfusion: How China and America Became One Economy and Why the World's Prosperity Depends on It.* New York, NY: Simon & Schuster, 2009.
Paul Krugman	*The Return of Depression Economics and the Crisis of 2008.* New York, NY: W.W. Norton, 2009.
Hunter Lewis	*Where Keynes Went Wrong: And Why World Governments Keep Creating Inflation, Bubbles and Busts.* Mount Jackson, VA: Axios Press, 2011.
Barry J. Naughton	*The Chinese Economy: Transitions and Growth.* Cambridge, MA: MIT Press, 2007.

Robert Paarlberg — *Food Politics: What Everyone Needs to Know*. New York: Oxford University Press, 2010.

Ron Paul — *End the Fed*. New York: Grand Central, 2009.

Robert B. Reich — *Aftershock: The Next Economy and America's Future*. New York: Vintage, 2011.

Carmen M. Reinhart — *This Time Is Different: Eight Centuries of Financial Folly*. Princeton, NJ: Princeton University Press, 2009.

Roberg J. Samuelson — *The Great Inflation and Its Aftermath: The Past and Future of American Affluence*. New York: Random House, 2008.

Peter D. Schiff and Andrew J. Schiff — *How an Economy Grows and Why It Crashes*. Hoboken, NJ: Wiley, 2010.

Nicholas Wapshott — *Keynes Hayek: The Clash That Defined Modern Economics*. New York, NY: W. W. Norton, 2011.

Donald R. Wells — *The Federal Reserve System: A History*. Jefferson, NC: McFarland, 2004.

David Wessel — *In FED We Trust: Ben Bernanke's War on the Great Panic*. New York, NY: Crown Publishing Group, 2009.

Patrick C. Westhoff — *The Economics of Food: How Feeding and Fueling the Planet Affects Food Prices.* Upper Saddle River, NJ: Pearson Education, 2010.

R. Christopher Whalen — *Inflated: How Money and Debt Built the American Dream.* Hoboken, NJ: John Wiley & Sons, 2011.

Index